THE SHARK INVESTOR

HOW TO APPLY "SHARK TANK" PRINCIPLES TO GETTING RICH IN THE STOCK MARKET

Michael W. Stern

Boston Finance Publishing

Boston Finance Publishing

Boston Finance Publishing is an imprint and trademark of Massinvestor, Inc. P.O. Box 142, Arlington, MA 02476

ISBN 979-8-9910013-0-4

FOR DEB, JOSH, AND HANNAH

THE SHARK INVESTOR

INTRODUCTION

THE SHARK INVESTOR IS A PERSONAL FINANCE BOOK written to help individual investors discover the next NVIDIA, Apple, and Facebook leveraging the same principles utilized by "Shark Tank" investors. While the "Shark Tank" TV show focuses on venture capital-like investments in privately-held startups, *The Shark Investor* teaches that much of the investment wisdom distilled on "Shark Tank" can be utilized in public-market stock picking.

Thinking like a Venture Capitalist is where *The Shark Investor* gets started. The book explores the difficulty of beating the market averages, how to engage in proper asset allocation, and more. *The Shark Investor* serves as a one-stop shop for how to analyze and buy winning individual stocks, as well as discover market-beating equity ETFs.

Maybe you've bought some stocks but feel you need additional ideas on how to manage them. Maybe you've inherited a portfolio of equities and need ideas on how to prune a collection of legacy securities. Maybe you've spent your investment "career" buying mutual funds and ETFs, but are curious about trying your hand with individual picks. *The Shark Investor* should deliver a variety of ideas.

If you're less interested in individual stocks, *The Shark Investor* also serves as a guide for investors interested in learning more about equity ETFs, and their proper role in a diversified portfolio.

While written primarily for investors with a basic modicum of experience with the stock market, the book can also be utilized by beginning investors trying to understand how exposure to the stock market can be beneficial, as well as more sophisticated investors who feel frustrated in their approach to the market.

The book's origin rests in the courses I teach through various adult education classes in the Greater Boston area. One student– a former professor whose son was a mutual fund portfolio manager– remarked how much she enjoyed the course and encouraged me to write a book.

Huh– write a book? Could I do it? Did I have enough content and ideas to make it happen? I took a look at the PowerPoint slides from my courses and realized there were nearly 100 slides in the combined decks. That could be a good starting point. The slides were mostly filled with bullet points, which I utilized to guide my teaching narrative. Sure– why not? Let's write a book, and maybe publish it as an eBook.

The writing could be tedious at first, but after banging out 20 pages, the ideas started flowing and the fingers were firing away on the keyboard. After it looked like I could reach 200 pages, I began to contemplate developing the book into a full-scale, publishable personal finance offering, not simply an addendum to my investment advisory business. I spent hours browsing the business section of my local Barnes & Noble, trying to glean insights into previous publications in the space. Did I have something new to tell? Could *The Shark Investor* make a fresh contribution? As I skimmed through dozens and dozens of investment books, I became convinced that *The Shark Investor* could offer three unique and important contributions:

1) I have decades of experience teaching stock picking and general investing to individual investors, and by teaching one learns about how individual investors actually *behave* with their investments. As we'll discover in this book, *behavior* more than intellect will likely determine investing success. My years of experience listening to investors, hearing their questions, and observing how they tend to learn and approach the markets is unique. I have witnessed the tendencies of my students to focus on Meme stocks, penny stocks, and companies they often know nothing about. This book promulgates strategies to avoid these self-defeating investment pursuits, and instead develop critical thinking to improve one's stock picking prowess. Most professional investors who teach the public focus on taking advantage of their students: luring them into an options trading seminar, or Day Trading course, or ultimately selling them some dubious investment. In my years as a teacher of the markets, I have focused on empowering investors to make good decisions, not duping them into buying some other product.

2) As far as I'm aware, *The Shark Investor* is the only book in personal finance that delves deeply into *why* professional money managers underperform the market. We hear this fact bandied about quite often, but there is little written on the subject as to why money managers do so poorly. Understanding the why is the clearest path to improvement.

3) This is the only investment book that explores how the investment methodology displayed on the "Shark Tank" television show can be utilized by public-market investors. In early-stage private capital

investing, there are sometimes no financial statements and certainly no stock charts, thus a Venture Capitalist attunes their attention to the CEO, the business model, the product, and the competitive space. They try to peer into the future and make a judgment as to whether the CEO in front them has the vision and fortitude to build a world-class company. A stock picker can gain tremendous advantages by aligning their thinking with the "Shark Tank" Venture Capitalist: the "Shark Investor."

ACKNOWLEDGMENTS

I must thank my intern Zach Post who was incredibly valuable helping with innumerable essential tasks for the book's organization and marketing. Andy Waldrop and Jennifer White were indispensable with their consults regarding the design of the book. Cindy Annisa contributed fantastic infographics and assisted with the cover design. Business writer, Scott Channell, provided insightful and even inspirational advice on building the project. Lastly, I want to thank my wife for her endless patience as a Photoshop whiz, copyeditor, and sounding board.

TABLE OF CONTENTS

PART VI DO THIS AND FORGET ABOUT THAT

THE SHARK INVESTOR

Contents

PART I

WHAT'S SO GREAT ABOUT THE STOCK MARKET?

WHAT'S SO GREAT ABOUT THE STOCK MARKET YOU MIGHT ASK? Why is there a daily newspaper in the *Wall Street Journal* dedicated to covering the markets' ups and downs? And why is there a cable channel– CNBC– broadcasting minute by minute information about stocks and infinite opinions about their future prices? Why do we hear a closing price announced for something called the "Dow Jones Industrial Average" each night on the evening television news?

Well, the answer is pretty simple– because the stock market has provided the best long-term returns for investors.

The returns from equities (stocks) have outperformed all other 'easily accessible' asset classes, such as Fixed Income (e.g. CDs and Treasuries); as well as residential real estate and Gold. When I say easily accessible asset classes– I mean investment sectors that the average, individual investor can participate in.

NFL franchises have increased in value greater than stocks. Pat Bowlen purchased the Denver Broncos in 1984 for $78 million, and when he passed in 2019, his heirs sold the franchise to Walmart heirs for $4.65 billion. As impressive as that may seem, it works out to an 11.35% return per year, right in line with the average annualized return over 25 years for NFL franchises. That's about 1.5% better than the stock market's long term annualized return. But the average American is unable to participate in the billionaire's world of sports franchises.

What about the dizzying values Impressionist art commands? Surely a Monet is a better investment than stocks, right? Not necessarily. According to data from ArtTactic (a provider of art market data), the stock market's returns easily best the 5.3% annualized return for Impressionist works (with an average holding period of 28 years for the art sub-group).

If you had invested $1 in the S&P 500 on Jan. 1, 1966, and reinvested all dividends, you would have ended up with approximately $100.00 at the end of market trading on Dec. 31, 2015.

That's 100 times your money over a 50-year time-span– an average annualized return of around 9.70%

Since the Great Depression, stocks have averaged 9.59% annual returns. That's 40% more than the bond market's average annual return. What about real estate? Stocks have outperformed residential real estate by 2.4% on an annualized basis. And let's be honest, home ownership can be out of reach for many Americans.

The annualized return from Gold isn't even close. From 1990 to 2020, the price of Gold increased by around 360%. Over the same period, the Dow Jones Industrial Average (DJIA) gained 991%.

The stock market– with recent advancements in fractional share purchases offered by brokerage firms like Robinhood– is the easiest way for most people to gain access to an investment class with returns significantly above a bank's savings rate and the rate of inflation.

Anyone can buy stocks! Even with just a small amount of money.

If I asked you, "What do you think $100.00 invested in the stock market in 1928 grew to by 2018," what would be your answer? If you wanted a few more parameters, by "stock market" I'm referring to the S&P 500.

And when we say the S&P 500, we mean an unmanaged index of 500 of the largest U.S. corporations. So, not buying low and selling high, or picking the best companies, or using options or margin (borrowing money). I'm talking plain vanilla: buying the index one time and leaving it alone. There are no buy and sell alterations other than investing all dividends back into the index.

So, this would be investing $100.00 in the S&P, leaving it alone for 90 years. Would you think it would have grown to $50,000? $100,000?

Let's add to your knowledge that by 1932 (post the stock market crash of 1929 and mired in the ensuing Great Depression), your $100.00 would have declined to $50.00. So, let's rephrase the question: "What did $50.00 in 1932 grow to by the end of 2018?

Now you're thinking maybe $25,000 or $50,000?

Sorry folks—but you'd be way below the correct figure. It's an astounding statistic that $50.00 invested in the S&P 500 in 1932 would have grown to $382,000 by 2018.

That's 90 years of incredible performance!

Perhaps the only statistic more impressive is that by the end of 2021, the $382,000 would have doubled to more than $760,000!

And what would that $100.00 have attained if you had invested in Gold? According to research from the NYU Stern School of business, $100.00 invested in Gold in 1928 would have grown to $8,800. If you invested in T-Bills (shorter duration government securities), the $100.00 grows to about $2,100. T-Bonds– longer duration government securities– produces about $8,500. How about corporate bonds? A little over $53,000. And surprisingly, Real Estate produced returns less than government bonds.

Those dazzling stock market returns were NOT through active trading. There was no genius involved. The only genius was holding onto the S&P 500 for many decades!

Ninety years sounds too long? Here's some more recent data: $15,500 invested in the S&P 500 in 1985 grew to $760,000 by 2021. That's nearly 50x the initial investment in 36 years.

What is This Thing Called the S&P 500?

On your nightly newscast you hear mostly about crimes, fires, sports, and weather, but there is usually a brief piece of business information offered: the day's performance of the Dow Jones Industrial Average. We are all familiar with the baritone voice declaring something like this: "Today the Dow Jones Industrial Average finished at 33,462– an increase of 342 points."

The Dow Jones Industrial Average is an index of 30 large U.S. companies, and the number that gets quoted on the evening news is essentially an average price for those 30 firms. It thus acts as a barometer of stock market performance.

While the Dow Jones Industrial Average is the most popularly quoted index, within the financial services industry, it is the S&P 500 that is the standard benchmark index. Professionals will talk more about the S&P

than "the Dow."

The S&P 500 Index is a market-capitalization-weighted index of the 500 largest U.S. publicly traded companies. If you don't know what market-capitalization means– don't worry– we'll get to it in a minute. The S&P 500 index is widely regarded as the single best gauge of the performance of large U.S. equities. It captures nearly 80% of the U.S. stock market's total value.

Other common U.S. stock market benchmarks include the Nasdaq Composite, which represents most Nasdaq issues; the S&P MidCap 400 Index, covering medium sized companies; and the Russell 2000 Index, which represents small-cap stocks.

If you want to judge the performance of your mutual fund manager, your stock broker, or your investment adviser– you should compare their returns to the S&P 500 Index.

What Percentage of Fund Managers Outperform the S&P 500?

"Alpha" is industry parlance for beating the S&P 500. On Wall Street, we have numerous professional money managers who buy and sell stocks based on what they think are the companies most likely to perform well. And if they can beat the performance of the S&P 500, they are handsomely rewarded. So, what percentage of fund managers achieve Alpha?

According to multiple studies, professional money managers consistently underperform the market average. According to *Fortune*, more than six in 10 actively managed stock funds were outperformed by their market benchmarks in 2016: "Large-cap funds failed to keep up with the S&P 500 66% of the time, while mid- and small-cap funds were outperformed by their benchmarks 89.3% and 85.5% of the time, respectively."

So, that was just one year– what about for longer time periods? The study cited by *Fortune* continued: "As bad as those numbers are, they only get worse over longer timelines. The overwhelming majority of all domestic funds were outperformed by their benchmarks over 1-, 3-, 5-, 10-, and 15-year intervals that ended December 2016."

The article continued: "Over the longest span, the numbers were particularly brutal. The S&P 500 outperformed more than 92% of large-cap funds over the last 15 years. Mid- and small-cap funds fared no better over the time period, with their benchmarks besting them 95.4% and 93.2% of the time, respectively."

But wait a minute– what about the winning managers you ask? After all, it's not 100% that underperform. What if an investor were to focus on the managers that have beaten the market? Isn't a portfolio manager's performance analogous to the output of an NFL running back or an NBA star? NFL rushers who ran for 1,000 yards their first few seasons typically run for 1,000 yards their next three seasons, right?

According to a CNBC article citing research from S&P Dow Jones Indices, you can't count on a winning manager to continue to outperform: "Analysts found that active fund managers who outperform their benchmark in one year struggle to get similar gains in the following years."

Unfortunately, the study found: "Only 5 percent of mutual funds that invest in large U.S. companies that had a winning three-year record against the S&P 500, continued to beat their benchmark in the three following years. The research shows that investors are not served well by chasing managers with great three-year track records."

If Lebron James averaged 25 points a game for three seasons in a row, there is a strong chance he'll score 25 the next three. But in money management, regression to the mean is the story of the day, not repeat outperformance.

Why Can't Fund Managers Beat the S&P 500?

As we've noted, professional investors actively managing a stock fund rarely exceed (over long periods of time) the returns of a passively managed fund owning the equities that comprise the S&P 500.

Ever wonder *why* fund managers can't beat the S&P 500? If this isn't the $1 trillion dollar question, I'm not sure what is?

In the movie "Wall Street" (which by the way, is the best business movie ever made), Michael Douglas' character Gordon Gekko answers the question by saying: "Because they're sheep, and sheep get slaughtered."

That's a clever quip, but really– why? Why can't all of the brilliant, well-trained, often Ivy-pedigreed, highly-compensated fund managers do better than a passively-managed index?

You'd think it would be the most pressing topic covered in financial media– but oddly it's not. In all my years of following the markets, I've only come across one article that wanted to tackle this $1 trillion dollar question– a 2019 column published in *Kiplinger Personal Finance* magazine.

The article cited a report authored by researchers at the University of Chicago, Carnegie Mellon University, the Massachusetts Institute of Technology, and data analysis firm Inalytics.

According to the *Kiplinger* article, the researchers considered an exhaustive amount of data: "They looked at 4.4 million trades for 783 portfolios run by professional money managers between 2000 and 2016. These were cream-of-the-crop managers, with portfolios averaging $573 million."

The study cited by *Kiplinger* found that the investment managers actually did a pretty good job of picking stocks. Their portfolios– for a while– did beat the S&P 500.

"The stocks that the managers added to their portfolios did well, outperforming the portfolios' benchmarks." That means a typical growth portfolio managers' discipline of buying stocks that are, let's say: growing earnings at 15%, have limited debt, have strong profit margins, et cetera… indeed, these strategies can result in performance that exceeds the returns of the unmanaged S&P 500 index.

So– what was the problem? If portfolio managers are picking winning stocks, why don't their returns exceed the S&P 500? ANSWER: The portfolio managers sold their stocks too quickly. "The managers' selling decisions, however, failed by a wide margin to beat even a zero-skill strategy of selling different, randomly chosen stocks in the portfolio."

"Rather than focus on, say, the outlook for profits or other fundamental measures of a company's prospects, the managers tended to sell their biggest losers or their biggest gainers. Portfolio managers who sold stocks with the most extreme returns fared the worst."

Thus, not only did the managers sell their winners too quickly, but they sold their losers too quickly as well.

It's almost easy to envision the mindset of the typical portfolio manager and the dilemmas presented by both winning and losing stocks. When one is up, the tendency is to sell and lock in profits. After all, there is the old industry adage that "Bulls make money, Bears make money, but pigs get slaughtered." In fact, let's go easy on these folks– it takes a lot of gumption to hold onto a stock that is up 2x, 4x, 10x and say– "I'm not going to sell."

This is where the index fund– by default– has the advantage. Unlike an active manager, the index manager doesn't have to ask the question– is it time to take profits? Remember, a portfolio that mimics the S&P 500 index NEVER sells its holdings, unless a company is removed from the index.

If a stock doubles, an active portfolio manager is tempted to take profits. And forget about doubling– many managers might think of a 20% to 30% gain as so titillating they would feel compelled to "lock in" their profits for the year.

This is quite different than a passive index. A stock can double and triple or go up 30x in value and there is NO PROFIT TAKING. As long as a particular security is a member of the S&P 500, it remains in the index and constitutes a larger piece of the index fund's total market value. When NVIDIA moved rapidly in 2023-2024 from a $300 billion market cap to a $3 trillion market cap, an active manager would scratch his or her head wondering when they should take profits. The index fund simply *holds* for the duration, capitalizing on this incredible upward surge in value.

We can also predict the behavior of the manager when a stock is down. No one likes losses. In fact, there are many strategies published suggesting an investor immediately cut losses at relatively small percentage intervals– like being down 5%.

The professional portfolio manager instinctively wants to cut their losses. But last year's loser stock might be next year's darling. Companies that have a poor earnings quarter, or poor year of earnings, typically find ways to improve. They might sell a weak division, find a new CEO, introduce a new product or service. Companies constantly evolve, and a punishing current year may lead to significant restructuring catalyzing future years of outperformance.

The research suggests managers don't employ the same discipline they have for selling as they do for buying. Buying may be the result of substantial research and analysis. But sell decisions are the result of significantly less due diligence.

Can I Really Get a Leg Up on Wall Street?

If professional portfolio managers have such a hard time beating the market, should an amateur investor even contemplate picking individual stocks? Yes– and one simple strategy the individual can employ is to hold stocks for longer periods of time than fund managers.

According to research by David Hunkar, a financial services consultant, stocks are typically held for less than a year. Citing studies from MFS

Investment Management as well as Ned Davis Research, Hunkar notes the following: "Stocks are being held for shorter periods than at any time since the 1920s. On average, a stock is being held for 8.3 months, less than a year."

If companies like Amazon, Netflix, Apple, Google and Microsoft have provided investors with long term average annualized returns of 20% to 30%, what would possibly be the benefit of holding one of these stocks for such a short period?

Forbes echoed Hunkar's comments citing research from Barclays and Novus. In a 2019 article on hedge funds, *Forbes* noted that most hedge funds typically hold their positions for nine months to a year.

Beat the Street by Not Being "Trigger Happy"

Money managers are notoriously impatient. According to research cited by the Institute of Business & Finance, the typical Large Cap Growth mutual fund has a turnover ratio of 70%. That means the typical manager (of this fund variety) sells roughly 2/3 of the companies he or she bought within the same calendar year! This screams out a significant lack of conviction.

Small Cap Growth managers engage in even a higher degree of trigger-happy behavior, jettisoning around 80% of their holdings within one year of purchase. Research by Morningstar indicated the average turnover ratio for managed domestic stock funds was 63% in 2019.

Warren Buffett, who we will discuss throughout this book, engages in the exact opposite behavior. Known as the greatest stock market investor, Buffett buys stocks with bountiful certitude, and often considers his purchases permanent holdings. Many companies in his portfolio, such as Coca-Cola, American Express, and Johnson and Johnson– he has held for decades.

Buffett started investing in stocks at the age of 11, but 99.7% of Buffett's wealth was earned after the age of 52.

That defines patience!

> **"The Stock Market is a device for transferring money from the impatient to the patient."**
>
> *-Warren Buffett*

Amazon founder Jeff Bezos– who joins Buffett among the richest men in the world– asked Buffett an important question: "…your style of investing is so simple, why doesn't everyone just copy you?"

Buffett's simple and incisive reply: "Because nobody wants to get rich slowly."

How Do I Pick The Right 9 to 12 Month Period? Don't!

How do I pick the right 9-12 month holding period? I ask this question facetiously. In order to put yourself in a position to exceed the returns of the professionals, you're going to need to focus on longer term investing. After all, what's the point in owning a fast-growing company for just 9-12 months? In order to participate in the long-term growth of a company, you have to own it long-term. One year rocket ships like NVIDIA in 2023-2024 are rare. Most of the great stock picks are stories that take time to develop.

In this chart studying 10-year returns, Amazon has advanced more than

1,000x, and Apple 940x. Would you be better off owning Amazon and Apple for some 9-12-month period (like the typical portfolio manager), or 9-12 years; or maybe 12-20 years?

	Price 6/20/14	Price 6/20/24	Annualized Gain	Total Gain
Amazon	$16.21	$186.10	27.64%	1,048.06%
Apple	$20.08	$209.44	26.42%	943.03%

Source: Yahoo Finance!

CASE IN POINT: On March 26th of 2024 I was watching CNBC and Stephanie Link, a portfolio manager and frequent guest on the network, was asked by CNBC's Scott Wapner why she had recently sold her position in paint retailer Sherwin-Williams. Link had appeared on the same show just a few weeks earlier extolling myriad characteristics of Sherwin-Williams. Housing was one of her favorite sectors, and paint was at the top of her list! Of course, Wapner challenged her on why she sold the stock; her one-line explanation was that the shares were up 20%.

Sherwin-Williams (NYSE:SHW) shares started the millennium at under $6.00 a share, and currently trade north of $360.00. It's one of the great growth stocks of the last 25 years– a 60-bagger! If she's so bullish on housing, why not own Sherwin-Williams for the next decade? Yet Link was satisfied with exiting at just a 20% gain.

The evidence is clear: portfolio managers are way too quick to take profits. The pressure to show strong quarterly and annual gains makes them far too trigger happy. Very few of them actually have a discipline for selling.

If you can exhibit patience like Warren Buffett, you can do better!

Individual Stocks Can Dramatically Outpace the S&P

Let's be clear, the vast majority of the funds you allocate to equities should be invested in Index ETFs. You'll take on far too much risk if most of your equity portfolio is in individual stocks.

But there is a case for buying individual equities. While 60% of the stocks that comprise the S&P 500 will likely *underperform* the S&P over a 10-year period, there will also be a handful of stocks that will dramatically outperform. And if you're able to invest in one of these outperformers, you could make a small fortune.

Take a look at the neighboring chart, which displays the performance of the S&P over the last 10 years relative to Apple, Amazon, Netflix, Google, and Facebook.

	Price 6/20/2014	Price 6/20/24	Annualized Gain	Total Gain
Amazon	$16.21	$186.10	27.64%	1,048.06%
Apple	$20.08	$209.44	26.42%	943.03%
Google (Alphabet)	$27.71	$177.71	20.42%	541.32%
Facebook (META)	$64.37	$501.70	22.79%	679.40%
Netflix	$62.88	$679.03	26.86%	979.88%
IVV (S&P 500 ETF)	$164.84	$547.94	12.76%	232.41%

Source: Yahoo Finance!

In that time period, the S&P posted a 232% total return, which is pretty impressive. But Google trumped the S&P with a 540% return (more than double the S&P). Not to be outdone, Facebook showcased a 679% return. Apple topped Facebook with a 943% return. Netflix shot up 979%, and

Amazon eclipsed them all with a 1,048% total return.

All of these stocks beat the S&P by wide margins. But the most important thing is that *none* of these companies were exotic names in this time period. Probably every reader of this book was utilizing a product or service from this group of companies. They weren't biotechs on the verge a monumental cure. They weren't alternative energy companies with a breakthrough technology. No flying cars. No 3D printing. No nascent industries. They were all multi-billion dollar businesses that we all utilized, understood, probably loved their products, and could have bought stock in.

...And You Don't Have to Buy Hot Tech Stocks!

If you're thinking: "Sure– Google, Netflix, Amazon, Apple, and Facebook all beat the S&P 500, but that means I've got to buy high-flying technology companies" – you would be incorrect.

Everyday, easy-to-understand consumer stocks such as Chipotle, Abercrombie & Fitch, and Dick's Sporting Goods all have dramatically outperformed the S&P over the last five years. Does anyone shop at Dick's or eat at Chipotle? Dick's Sporting Goods is up nearly 500% the last five years, and Chipotle is up 230%; while the S&P is up a seemingly paltry 101%.

Have you ever shopped at Ulta Beauty for cosmetics?

Did you consider investing in the stock?

Ulta Beauty shares are up about 50-fold over the last 15 years!

Do you want to guess what the best performing stock has been over the last 30 years? NVIDIA, Apple, Microsoft? Wrong!

THE SHARK INVESTOR
WHAT'S SO GREAT ABOUT THE STOCK MARKET?

It's Monster Beverage– the highly caffeinated energy drink whose stock has appreciated by about 200,000% since 1994. And by the way– speaking of boring names (as we'll soon discuss with Peter Lynch)– the original company name for Monster was Hansen's Natural Sodas.

So, you don't have to find the newest technology, a breakthrough biotech, or a dazzling new product.

Burritos, cosmetics, beverages, apparel, and sporting goods are everyday products that you are probably consuming and using right now– and you can grow rich by participating in the growth of the companies behind them.

NOTE: The S&P 500 Index was first developed in 1957, and grew out of a predecessor S&P Composite Index created in 1926 with 90 stocks.

PART II

THINKING LIKE A SHARK

HOW DO VENTURE CAPITALISTS GET RICH? Venture Capitalists don't come up with great ideas! They find entrepreneurs with great ideas and supply them capital.

They invest in illiquid startup businesses often at preposterous valuations. I say preposterous because seed stage investments are generally made in companies with little to no revenue, and early stage investments are made in companies at staggering multiples of revenue.

A startup that actually has $1 million in revenues may receive a $10 million equity investment valuing the company at $50 million. 50x sales in the world of publicly-traded companies would be a "Nosebleed Valuation," attracting the attention of short sellers.

But Venture Capitalists perform significant due diligence (research) on the product, the market, and the entrepreneur.

And they hold their investments for many years, shepherding a company from a seed or early stage to more mature stages, and in some cases to an Initial Public Offering.

A stock market investor should train themselves to think like a Venture

THE SHARK INVESTOR
THINKING LIKE A SHARK

Capitalist. Venture Capitalists meet entrepreneurs and learn about their ideas. They hear the startup "pitch," and they ask important questions:

What will the future look like for this startup? What's the addressable market size?

Is this Entrepreneur/ CEO capable of building a large, important company?

Can this product/ service be useful for many years to come?

Can it grow its business at 50% to 100% for 5-10 years?

Venture Capitalists "Ride the Coattails" of great entrepreneurs and businesses. The average investor may not get to see what goes on during an entrepreneurial pitch at a VC firm. However, they can get a strong idea of the process that VCs undertake in scrutinizing potential investments by watching television's "Shark Tank" program.

"Shark Tank" is a wildly popular show airing on ABC with reruns appearing several times a week on CNBC. Entrepreneurs pitch their ideas to a panel of "Sharks"– all successful businessmen and women– in hopes of receiving a seed stage investment.

Can stock market investors learn something from these "Sharks"? Absolutely! In fact, a stock market investor *should* apply the same discipline to prospective investments as the "Sharks" demonstrate.

When I say discipline– I mean investigating a prospective company in the same manner that the "Sharks" query the entrepreneurs that seek their dollars.

Let me break the news to you– the stock market is not like Las Vegas! Stock prices increase in value because of strong earnings. And strong earnings are the result of great products, great business models, and great leadership.

Just as "Shark" Lori Greiner says she looks for "heroes" in her private company investing, investors should look for heroes in their public market investing.

On "Shark Tank," you see the "Sharks" scrutinize products, business plans, and entrepreneurs.

These are three very different and very important items to analyze.

YOU want to look for hero products and business models.

And YOU want to look for hero entrepreneurs.

YOU want to be the chief "Shark" of the stocks you consider investing in. Think of researching your prospective portfolio companies with the same level of scrutiny demonstrated by the "TV Sharks."

If you've never watched an episode of "Shark Tank"– I strongly recommend doing so. It will help you hone your business and investing chops. Or, put differently– sharpen your "Shark" investment teeth.

"Stay in Your Lane" Like Daymond John and Lori Greiner

In what industry did "Shark" Daymond John make his money? Fashion. John started off selling hand-sewn, wool ski hats on the streets of Queens, New York in 1992. In order to grow the fledgling business, his mother took out a second mortgage on their home and backed her entrepreneurial son. Daymond's mom was a shrewd investor: as of 2024, his apparel brand FUBU has raked in $6

billion in worldwide sales.

If you notice, Daymond doesn't invest in too many opportunities that aren't fashion or apparel oriented.

Lori Greiner, a consumer products entrepreneur known for her show on shopping channel QVC, focuses on household products that solve problems and can be advertised on QVC. Period. She'll routinely pass on startups she considers outside her wheelhouse.

For you as an investor, this means simplifying the number of industries you consider investing in. Make sure that you have some experience with, and knowledge of, a prospective company and its market.

There is no need for you to invest in oil services companies if that is an industry you know nothing about.

What industry do you work in? What's your area of expertise? Where do you shop? What services do you consume regularly? What products do you love? By asking yourself these questions, you might start identifying companies that could turn out to be great investments.

Another key way to think of the investment process is this: Don't invest in a company unless you have bought the product, used the service, and tried one of the competitors' products or services.

I guarantee you– when you invest in companies that you know nothing about in industries you don't understand, you'll have a hard time stomaching Bear markets. When the stock drops 30% and the only reason you bought the company was because you got a tip from a friend or a post on Reddit, you'll feel like you're on a sinking ship.

Remember– think of yourself as the Analyst or the Venture Capitalist. YOU are the information gatherer and decision maker. You're the "Shark." Make yourself an expert on your prospective company, not a follower of others.

Don't Obsess Over Current Valuation Like "Mr. Wonderful"

A Canadian-born businessman, Kevin O'Leary made a small fortune rolling up educational software companies and unloading the package to Mattel for billions of dollars in 1999. Capable of waxing eloquently on guitars, wines, and photography, O'Leary's current business interests include a family of investment funds (O'Shares) as well as a venture capital fund (O'Leary Ventures).

His business acumen is remarkable, however, a glaring mistake of O'Leary's is that he obsesses over the current valuations of the startups presenting on "Shark Tank." O'Leary, who refers to himself as "Mr. Wonderful," routinely pounds presenting entrepreneurs over the head with criticisms of their startup's valuation, often to the chagrin of the other "Sharks." In O'Leary's mind, a startup should be valued the

same way as a mature business. When presenting startups don't submit to his draconian valuations, he often declares: "You're dead to me."

O'Leary is shrewd, no doubt. However, a seed-stage Venture Capitalist will routinely invest in companies that have no or minimal revenues, and of course no profits.

Venture Capitalists often award valuations of tens of millions to money-losing, early-stage startups; and then hundreds of millions or even billions for still-unprofitable, later-stage startups. Uber, as an example was founded in 2009, and raised more than $32 billion as an unprofitable enterprise. The ride hailing service went public in 2019 but didn't turn a profit until 2023.

You want to think like a Venture Capitalist. Not because they take enormous risks, but because of their capacity to peer into the future. They stare at products and business models and entrepreneurs and they ask: "What is the Total Addressable Market? Does this entrepreneur seem like someone who can build a successful enterprise? Can I imagine a company 10x, 100x, 1,000x bigger than what I see now?"

Remember– companies evolve. Amazon started as a bookstore. Then they started selling practically everything. Then they added Web Services. Then they acquired Whole Foods.

A great entrepreneur will lead a company far past its present state, and a company will grow as the vision of the CEO progresses.

A current valuation for a company may seem high, but don't get completely bogged down like Mr. Wonderful. Companies grow organically, buy out competitors, and add new divisions. They can grow into optimistic present-day valuations.

Barbara Corcoran: People Person

I can't overemphasize understanding CEO talent enough, and reading people is Barbara Corcoran's main focus.

Corcoran, who made her money as one of New York City's top real estate brokers, will consider investing in companies with products she doesn't understand or maybe doesn't even like. But if the entrepreneur arouses her investor appetite, she will overlook the product deficiencies and pounce to invest.

Comfy (a sweatshirt/ blanket combo) was a product she claims she didn't even understand. But she liked the entrepreneurs and invested, and Comfy has turned out to be her best investment from "Shark Tank." Her $50,000 outlay for one third of the company has netted her over $450 million.

According to a CNBC article (quoting the podcast "Chicks in the Office"), Corcoran said she's at the point in her tenure on the show where she isn't impressed with products and services anymore, but will be wooed by the business owners themselves.

"The No. 1 trait I'm looking for

"Her ability to recognize the good and bad in somebody, what they'll be like as an entrepreneur, what they'll be like as a person – Barbara picks up on that stuff in a minute."

-Mark Cuban

[is] ambition," Corcoran explained. "Someone who envisions where they're going, and I fall for it when they tell me they're going there."

For the individual investor, that means trying to gather intelligence on the CEO of a prospective investment: reading magazine articles in *Forbes* or *Fortune*; finding web articles at *Business Insider, Bloomberg, CNNMoney*; or maybe you'll catch an interview on CNBC.

Bottom line is this– in order to find the next Amazon, you'll need to identify the next Jeff Bezos. To get the returns of NVIDIA, you'll need to find a Jensen Huang.

Mark Cuban: The Visionary

Mark Cuban, with a net worth of $6.2 billion, is the wealthiest of all the "Sharks." Cuban, who sold a profitless startup to Yahoo! for $5.7 billion in 1999, does the best job of looking into the future. He routinely dismisses "Mr. Wonderful's" obsession with valuation and current revenue numbers, and instead focuses on the entrepreneur and potential business growth.

When BeatBox appeared on "Shark Tank" in 2014 pitching their packaged wine product, the startup whetted the appetite of a few "Sharks." Kevin O'Leary offered an investment equivalent to what the BeatBox entrepreneurs were seeking, which valued the firm at $2 million. Yet

Cuban trumped the other "Sharks" by offering an investment valuing BeatBox at $3 million, which the company's founders accepted. BeatBox only had $235K in sales at that point, and "Mr. Wonderful" shook his head in disbelief at Cuban's bountiful offer.

But Cuban assessed BeatBox as a company that didn't just sell wine, but also sold fun, and his aggressive investment paid off. The business is now doing in excess of $20 million in sales annually, and in 2022 raised $15 million from private investors at a $200 million valuation; more than 60x the generous valuation that Cuban paid.

Remember, current and past revenues are important to know about, but they are not the future. Cuban looked beyond present revenues and envisioned a much larger company.

As an investor, you're interested in *future* revenues and profits. That's why "Fundamental Analysis," which looks at the balance sheet and income statement, won't tell you if a company will perform well in the next twelve months or the next five years.

You must contemplate any business and stock from the "Top Down"– meaning you have to think about the entire market in which a company is competing in. We'll talk more about this when we get to "Top Down Analysis" in a later chapter.

Robert Herjavec: People Person II

Another Canadian businessman, Robert Herjavec founded BRAK Systems, an integrator of internet security software, and sold it to AT&T Canada in 2000 for $30.2 million. His current IT operation, The Herjavec Group, does $200 million in annual revenues.

THE SHARK INVESTOR
THINKING LIKE A SHARK

Like Barbara Corcoran, Herjavec is less interested in the current state of affairs of a product or business, and instead trains his attention on the founder giving him the pitch. "A great entrepreneur can take a so-so product and make a great business out of it. A bad entrepreneur can take a great product and run it into the ground," Herjavec explains. "Bet on the jockey, not on the horse."

You need to know who the "jockey" is of a company you're considering buying stock in. Doesn't that make sense? You're going to be entrusting your dollars to his or her decisions. Who is the CEO? How long have they been with the company? Is the CEO the founding entrepreneur? How much stock do they own?

Great CEOs can transform businesses almost like magic. Waste Management is the largest garbage collection company in the world, yet today's Waste Management began with one man– Wayne Huizenga– who started collecting garbage with a single truck in the 1960s in South Florida. Yes– he was not a "corporate suit"– *he was the garbage man*!

"A great entrepreneur can take a so-so product and make a great business out of it. A bad entrepreneur can take a great product and run it into the ground. Bet on the jockey, not on the horse."

After he left Waste Management, Huizenga dabbled in some different investments and stumbled across a video rental chain in Dallas called Blockbuster. He took a controlling stake in Blockbuster and built it into the largest video rental chain in the world.

After selling Blockbuster to Viacom (now Paramount) for billions, he then decided to get back into garbage, and built the country's third biggest waste removal company Republic Services.

While he was building Republic, Huizenga was also buying auto dealerships, and then later spun out his consolidated auto acquisitions into the largest automobile dealership in the world– AutoNation.

ONE MAN built all of these industry leading businesses in different verticals. You want to find Wayne Huizengas and ride their coattails. Know thy CEO!

Chris Sacca: Spread Your Bets

Though pictured here in a tuxedo, oft cowboy-shirt-wearing Chris Sacca has appeared on multiple "Shark Tank" episodes as a guest investor. A billionaire Venture Capitalist from Silicon Valley, Sacca made his fortune with early bets on Uber, Twitter, and Instagram.

Sacca is perfectly comfortable with risk, but it's highly calculated, and his insights into venture investing are perfectly applicable to public market

THE SHARK INVESTOR
THINKING LIKE A SHARK

---

investing.

"Only invest what you can lose. Don't borrow," Sacca once said in an interview with *Markets Insider*. "Spread it around multiple investments. And, overall, assume you are going to lose your money and be pleasantly surprised if you get back more than you put in. Good luck."

You're in luck– Sacca's comments about "losing" your money are less relevant for public markets– as stocks rarely go to zero. Venture Capital investments often go to zero.

But his comments on avoiding margin (borrowing money) and spreading your risk around are immensely applicable. We'll talk more about developing your portfolio when we discuss the "Spray and Pray" strategy, as well as eschewing margin in a later chapter.

SUMMARY: The Shark Thesis

When you're seeking out the next Amazon, Google, Facebook, or Starbucks utilize the same discovery process as the "Sharks." Your line of inquiry will include understanding the valuation, the business model, the opportunity, and the CEO.

It will probably be necessary NOT to focus on buying deeply undervalued securities. In fact, it might be necessary to buy a stock at a valuation that appears a little expensive. *But*, you will avoid buying at "Nosebleed Valuations" (which we'll discuss in a later chapter).

You'll want revenues to be growing briskly: target firms with revenue growth of 20%+.

You will focus on buying companies in durable markets.

You will perform substantial due diligence on the CEO. What drives them? How do they treat employees? Are they considered a product visionary? What is their ownership stake in the company?

You will stay abreast of the overall market that your company competes in. Who are the competitors? What differentiates your prospective investment from the competition? How will they maintain pricing power? What problem does the firm you're considering investing in solve? Why do the firm's customers *need* the product or service?

In a client newsletter (excerpted and published at *Insider Monkey*), investment firm Saga Partners issued a well-articulated investment thesis for the stock The Trade Desk (Nasdaq:TTD), a digital advertising platform. The analysis sums up many of the company attributes a "Shark" investor would seek out.

"The Trade Desk is truly an exceptional company. Its platform helps advertisers comb through a huge universe of possible ad inventory to target and value the token few that make sense for that specific advertiser. It is very rare to come across a company that has high and growing barriers to entry, economies of scale, network effects, and compounding demand. The cherry on top is that it is founder-led with management owning a significant number of shares that make up nearly their entire net worth."

I'm not necessarily endorsing The Trade Desk, but I'm endorsing the story the analyst communicates. For any stock you're going to consider purchasing, you'll need to identify the elements of the business that will make it successful. Build your story before you invest. We will explore these "Shark" principles of analyzing the valuation, business model, opportunity, and CEO throughout the book. And we will learn to build a "story" for why a prospective investment is likely to be fruitful.

THE SHARK INVESTOR

PART III

RESEARCHING INDIVIDUAL STOCKS

W HAT MAKES STOCKS GO UP? For some investors, the stock market simply feels like a casino. I remember in my Merrill Lynch days talking to a prospect who worked with a lot of different stockbrokers. He believed that brokers had hot streaks. And similar to a hot casino player rolling sevens at the craps table, he wanted to find a broker whose lucky streak he could leverage.

As I'll mention when I caution about Day Trading– an activity where investors get sucked in by the casino-like "bling" of flashing green and red lights and colorful moving charts and blinking numbers– this *gambling* mentality is unlikely to be productive.

Other investors become fixated on the short-term catalysts for stocks: domestic political swings, geopolitical events, industry news, competitor news, etc. In a given day or week, there are myriad micro-events that an investor could interpret as being impactful for their stock holdings. And they very well may be impactful in the short-term.

But long-term, we can safely say there is *one* factor that will ultimately cause stocks to increase or decrease in price: EARNINGS (profits). Please read this sentence again and deeply inculcate it. Increasing or decreasing profits/earnings/net income (all the same thing) will be the primary mover of stocks.

When a company's profits increase, it becomes more valuable. If a company grows from having $10 million in earnings to $1 billion in earnings, the company's stock should increase (roughly) 100x.

Let's take a look at NVIDIA, a company that makes a lot of news these days both for its industry impact and rising stock price. Before we get to profits, we'll take a look at revenue. A company's revenue generally advances in order to create rising profits. On February 17, 2010, NVIDIA reported year-end numbers with revenue of $3.3 billion and net income of $141 million. The stock price was a split-adjusted $.41 (forty-one cents).

In 2010, NVIDIA was known primarily as a develop of chips to power graphics in PCs, especially useful for gamers. Just prior to COVID, NVIDIA was garnering investor interest as the premier provider of chips to data centers that serve as backbones for cloud computing solutions. Post COVID, NVIDIA has generated buzz regarding how its chips are utilized to power Artificial Intelligence. What's important, is that in the last fourteen years, NVIDIA's influence in technology has grown by an extraordinary order of magnitude. In January of 2024, Facebook's Mark Zuckerberg indicated his company would be buying 350,000 NVIDIA graphics cards– a multi-billion-dollar investment– to power Meta's AI ambitions.

Business growth and influence is what investors should focus on first. Business growth will lead to increased revenues, which generally lead to increased profits, and the stock price will follow suit.

NVIDIA's 2024 annual revenues surpassed $60 billion. And many analysts foresee 2025 revenues hitting $90 billion.

NVIDIA	2020	2021	2022	2023	2024
Revenues	$10.9B	$16.7B	$26.9B	$26.9B	$60.9B
Profits	$2.8B	$4.3B	$9.8B	$4.4B	$29.7B

So, how has NVIDIA's stock price fared as its revenue has soared from under $4 billion (in 2010) to $60 billion, and net income raced from $141 million to $30 billion?

As of this writing, NVIDIA's shares are just above $120.00, a roughly 265-fold increase from 2010. Can you do better at a casino?

So, forget about the short-term events. A growing business with increasing earnings will propel a stock higher, ultimately dismissing health crises (COVID), geopolitical crises (Ukraine), interest rate crises, and other near-term calamities.

SPEAKING OF INTEREST RATES, while earnings movement ultimately catalyzes stock price movement, we cannot ignore interest rates. Let's consider it the second most impactful item for stock prices.

Interest rate changes can have a dramatic impact on the macro stock environment as well as an individual stock.

Remember– stocks compete with other investments for investor attention. In 1981 an investor could buy a 30-year Treasury yielding over 14%, more than 40% higher than the historical average return on stocks. If you can earn 14% risk free with a government Treasury, why take the risk in owning a volatile asset like stocks? That's why the Dow Jones hit

769 in 1981, down 25% from a peak set in 1966. Stocks simply weren't attractive compared with Treasury yields above 10%.

Rising interest rates also make the cost of capital higher for companies. When corporate borrowing costs are higher, it means less dollars make their way to the corporate bottom line (profits).

We don't have to look too far back in our memory banks to recognize the impact interest rate changes have on the market. Between 2018 and the end of 2021 the stock market doubled. The Federal Reserve began raising rates in March of 2022, and by the end of 2022 the S&P had dropped 18% and the Nasdaq was off 33%. In late October of 2023, yields on the 10-year Treasury brushed 5%, and the market swooned again. When investors could attain a 5.5% return in risk-free CDs and Treasuries, the stock market looked less appetizing.

In late 2023, falling inflation came to the market's rescue. In December, when Chairman Powell announced that the Federal Reserve saw current rates as potentially damaging to the economy and signaled rate cuts in 2024, the stock market soared.

The influence of the Federal Reserve, and its capacity to alter borrowing costs and fixed-income investment returns, leads to the investment wisdom: "Don't fight the Fed." While the powerful impact of the Fed should never be ignored, don't let it dominate your investment game plan. Your Asset Allocation strategy (see Section IX) should keep you in good stead through interest rate vicissitudes. And for your equity positions– including individual stock picks– long-term earnings growth should trump the impact of shorter-term interest rate moves.

Understanding Market Valuation

It's important to understand the valuation of a prospective investment. And valuation really means– how much does it cost? Now, I'm not talking about whether the share price is $1.00 or $50.00 or $500.00. The actual share price is meaningless. You need to know the market valuation or market capitalization (often shortened to market cap).

This means taking a quoted share price– say $50.00– and finding out how many shares the company has– known as "Shares Outstanding." In this context the word "outstanding" does not mean great. It simply means that the shares exist and are available for trading.

If a $50.00 stock has 1 million shares outstanding, then it has a $50 million dollar valuation in the market. So, if you wanted to buy all the shares, you'd need to pony up $50 million.

Does a company you're researching have 1 billion shares trading at $85.00 per share? Then it has an $85 billion dollar market cap.

Understanding the valuation of a company is no different than understanding the cost of a car or refrigerator or new TV you're considering buying. When you're thinking about buying a car, you don't contemplate its cost in terms of a fractional unit. When you go to the car dealership and look at the sticker price it will say $50,295; not $50.00 per share.

When you think about buying a stock, have some consideration for the *total* marketplace value of the company, not just its individual share price.

Once you've determined *what* the market cap of a prospective company is– $500 million, $5 billion, $50 billion– it will be important to grasp what bracket of market capitalization it falls under– meaning is it a large capitalization company, a Mid Cap, or a Small Cap? If you look

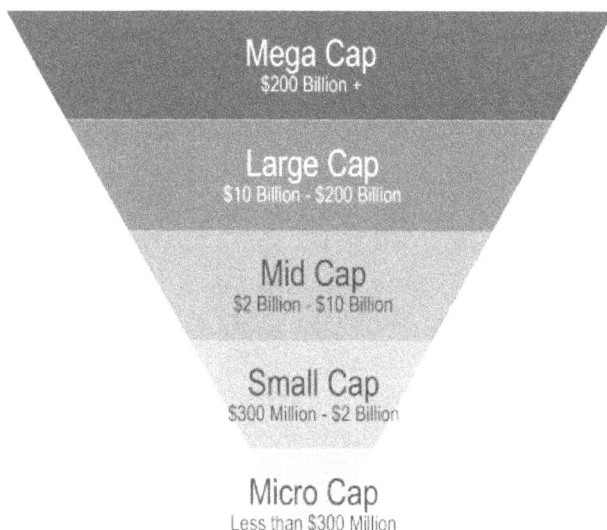

at the image above, we can see that companies will fit within five tiers of market capitalization. You might see someone else define a Small Cap as running up to a $1 billion level, but the strata presented in this figure are widely accepted definitions.

As of this writing, capturing market data from July 2024– Microsoft is the biggest market cap company with a $3.37 trillion dollar market value. Apple trails as a close second sporting a $3.32 trillion dollar value. NVIDIA, Google, and Amazon round out the top five, all with market caps above two trillion.

Many well-known companies that often make news are in the Mega Cap space such as NVIDIA, Tesla, Facebook, Google, Microsoft, Berkshire Hathaway, Apple, and Home Depot.

Also, many of the companies that make up the Dow Jones Industrial Average (30 companies) are Mega Cap names.

The S&P 500 index comprises the 500 largest market cap names, so obviously it will include all of the Mega Cap names, and Large Cap companies. Some of the smallest market cap names in the S&P 500 include Paramount Global (Nasdaq:PARA) with a $7.8 billion market cap, and American Airlines (NYSE:AAL) sporting a $7 billion valuation. So, technically there are some Mid Caps that make their way into the S&P 500.

MARKET CAP EXAMPLES

Microsoft	$3.28 Trillion	Mega Cap
Ralph Lauren	$11.35 Billion	Large Cap
Sweetgreen	$3.62 Billion	Mid Cap
JetBlue	$1.83 Billion	Small Cap
Nathan's	$280 Million	Micro Cap

Fundamental Analysis vs. Top-Down Analysis

Fundamental Analysis (also called Bottom-Up Analysis) is a method of evaluating a security in an attempt to assess its intrinsic value. A practitioner examines economic, financial, and other qualitative and quantitative factors. These include looking at financial statements, and utilizing ratios that analyze the price of the stock relative to sales and earnings; the overall return on assets and equity, and other financial metrics. Peter Lynch and Warren Buffet come to mind as two of the ultimate fundamental stock pickers. They performed extensive research on companies they invested in. They read annual reports, SEC filings, and visited companies. They invested because they were convinced that their dollars were buying excellent businesses capable of producing above average profits for years to come. We'll discuss important elements of Fundamental Analysis in successive chapters.

Top-Down Analysis looks at the "big picture" first. An investor who utilizes Top-Down analysis typically begins by analyzing the global economy. They then assess macro trends within industries and countries that they believe have the best opportunities. Finally, individual stocks within favorable sectors and regions are selected.

Perhaps the greatest Top-Down investor over the last number of decades is Jim Rogers, who helped power multi-billionaire George Soros' phenomenal returns. In 1973, Soros and Rogers both left an investment bank and co-founded the Quantum Fund. From 1973 to 1980, the fund gained 4,200% while the S&P advanced about 47%. One of the Quantum Funds' biggest bets was in oil stocks in the 1970s. In 1985 Rogers thought Portugal looked ripe for economic gains after the country fought off Communist influence. He instructed his investment agent to buy all 24 stocks on the Portugal exchange and every new issue that followed. He eventually owned 35 different positions with brilliant results. In the late 1990s when everyone was getting manic about tech stocks, Rogers made big bets in commodities as their prices had plummeted. By the time the dollar declined to extraordinary lows in 2007, Rogers' bets on commodities had skyrocketed. Around the same time he focused on commodities, Rogers became a huge bull on China due to its ballooning economy and global influence. He sold his New York City townhouse in 2007 for $15.75 million (which he had bought for around $100,000), moved to Singapore (enrolling his daughters in Mandarin classes), and made a killing in Chinese stocks.

These two schools of thought– Fundamental and Top-Down Analysis– should not be considered contrary, mutually exclusive disciplines. You will need Top-Down Analysis to be successful. Fundamental Analysis, while critical for understanding companies, only shows you the past! Cabletron and Bay Networks were amazing stocks in the early and mid-nineties, and all the fundamentals looked great when you explored their financial statements. But they simply didn't have the technological *chutzpah* to compete with Cisco (into the 2000s), and Cisco ultimately ate up their market share.

Skating to where the puck is going is far more critical than skating to where the puck is now or has been. Top-Down Analysis is akin to skating to where the puck is going.

Value Investing vs. Growth Investing

Value and Growth investing are two Fundamental approaches, or styles, in stock investing. Growth investors seek companies that offer strong earnings growth (generally growing at 15% or better); while Value investors seek stocks that appear to be undervalued in the marketplace.

We'll tackle Value investing first: a Value investor focuses on companies he/she believes are priced inaccurately by the market. They believe that through careful research and analysis they can create a model for the correct value for a company.

As an example, IDT (NYSE:IDT) was a company in which I invested in the early 2000s. A telecommunications outfit, IDT was known for their long-distance calling cards. They also built a Voice over IP technology

THE SHARK INVESTOR
RESEARCHING INDIVIDUAL STOCKS

branded as Net2Phone, a division they sold in 2000 to AT&T for $1.1 billion in cash. After the sale to AT&T, IDT was sitting on over $1 billion in cash but had a market cap of under $1 billion. They also had approximately $1 billion of annual revenue. This looked like a bargain to me—where a company was trading in the market at a valuation less than the cash on its balance sheet, and at an approximate 1:1 price to sales ratio.

Another simple method of finding a value is utilizing the PEG ratio (page 83). When a company is trading at a PE ratio (page 79) that is less than its growth rate, it can be considered undervalued.

A strict value investor will often employ the following precepts:

- **Fundamental Analysis:** Value investors rely significantly on Fundamental Analysis, which as we discussed, involves evaluating the financial health, performance, and prospects of a company. This analysis includes examining financial statements, assessing competitive advantages, management quality, and industry dynamics.
- **Intrinsic Value:** Value investors aim to determine the intrinsic value of an asset, which is its true worth based on its fundamentals, such as earnings, cash flow, and assets. They seek to invest in assets that are trading *below* their intrinsic value.
- **Margin of Safety:** Value investors emphasize the importance of having a margin of safety when investing. This means purchasing assets at a discount to their intrinsic value, providing a cushion against potential losses and market fluctuations.
- **Long-Term Perspective:** Value investing typically takes a long-term perspective, focusing on the underlying value and potential future growth of an asset rather than short-term market trends.

Value investors often exert profound patience, waiting for the market to recognize the true value of their investments.

These tenets were largely developed by Benjamin Graham, a Columbia University professor, who was Warren Buffett's mentor and author of the bibles of the discipline: *Security Analysis* (1934 with David Dodd); and *The Intelligent Investor* (1949).

Let's be clear, the type of orthodox Value investing that Graham preached– which favored buying companies at prices discounted below their Current Assets (see page 89)– is difficult to employ today. Most worthwhile companies simply don't trade at such discounted prices unless there are concerns over their capacity to stay in business.

Let's also emphasize that Value investing is not necessarily the opposite of Growth investing. In fact, the "Shark Investor" supposition holds that you'll want to employ both constructs: 1) You'll want to find companies that are growing their earnings briskly; 2) But you'll also need to pay a reasonable valuation for them. You don't need to seek out a Ben Graham-styled, deeply discounted valuation. But if you pay a "Nosebleed Valuation," (see page 167) it won't matter how much a company's earnings grow. Dramatically overvalued firms often incorporate a decade's worth of positive earnings growth, and are often considered great companies but bad stocks.

Always Buy Growth, And It's Not Bad If You Can Get Value as Well!

Princeton Economics professor Burton Malkiel isn't a big fan of individual stock picking. His erudite tome *A Random Walk Down Wall Street* is chalk full of arguments favoring index investing over individual stock selection.

However, he does make it very clear that if you are going to pick stocks, absolutely choose companies whose earnings are growing. His Rule #1 is quite explicit: "Buy only companies that are expected to have above-average earnings growth for five or more years. An extraordinary long-run earnings growth rate is the single most important element contributing to the success of most stock investments. Amazon, Netflix, and practically all the other really outstanding common stocks of the past were growth stocks."

It's pretty simple folks, when profits are declining, a company becomes less valuable. Assets don't mean anything if they can't produce profits. $10 billion in sales is far less significant than $10 billion in profits.

If a company's profits grow at a high rate for 10, 20, or even 30 years, then the company should become considerably more valuable. Successful stock market investing isn't any more complicated than this simple premise.

Here's some math: at the end of two decades of earnings growth of 15% per annum, a company that starts year one with $1 million in profits would grow to sporting more than $16 million in profits. 15% earnings growth may not sound like a torrid pace, but it's 50% higher than the long-term average of 9.8% earnings growth for the S&P 500.

And if a company's profits grow 16-fold, there is a good chance that the company's stock price will grow in a commensurate fashion.

I hope you noticed something powerfully important. The long-term earnings growth rate for the S&P 500 is 9.8%. And what is the 90-year stock market return? Just under 10%– almost a perfect match. Earnings growth begets stock price growth.

We just found the answer to successful investing! A company's stock price– long term– will likely correlate with its earnings growth. If you buy a company whose profits are growing at 5% per annum, don't expect to quadruple your money in 10 years. However, if you invest in a company growing earnings at 25% per year, you could potentially see your money double every few years.

THE SHARK INVESTOR

PART IV

THE WISDOM OF PETER LYNCH AND WARREN BUFFETT

FAMED MUTUAL FUND MANAGER PETER LYNCH over-saw Fidelity's Magellan fund between 1977 and 1990. During this 13-year period, the fund posted an annual average return of 29%, beating the S&P 500 index in 11 out of 13 years. During his tenure, Magellan's assets under management swelled from $18 million to $14 billion.

Lynch, whose father died when he was 10 years of age, decided to retire from money management before the age of 50, and spend more time with his wife and two daughters. By leaving the investment game early in his career, he doesn't have the multi-decade track record of Warren Buffett, nor a personal net worth in the multi-billions. But his performance at Fidelity places him in the all-star pantheon of professional managers.

Lynch's first book on investing, *One Up On Wall Street,* is a classic and a must-read for anyone looking to become a serious stock-picker. Besides offering incredibly sage advice, Lynch's wit is impressive as well.

THE SHARK INVESTOR
THE WISDOM OF PETER LYNCH & WARREN BUFFETT

Lynch is an excellent teacher, and a beginning investor can read his book and slowly dip their toes into understanding metrics like P/E ratio and Debt-to-Equity Ratio. He is able to glide into these concepts without making the reader feel they are taking a math class.

The most important take-away from Lynch's tome is that an individual investor's best strategy to compete with the Wall Street pro, is to home in on the companies, products, and stores around them. The book's subtitle is the key: "How to Use What You Already Know to Make Money in the Market."

Lynch's thesis is simple: rather than invest in a hot stock featured in a magazine or bandied about at a social gathering, an individual investor will likely do better by targeting businesses they frequent and understand.

You should read all of Lynch's classic *One Up On Wall Street*, but if you are short on time, here's a synopsis of Lynch's 13 principles for finding the "Perfect Stock." Some of Lynch's writing from his 1989 magnum opus sounds a bit dated 35 years later– such as his use of the term "cocktail party" as a common casual social event. I'm not sure what the modern equivalent to the cocktail party is– keg party, wine tasting, poker night, single malt scotch gathering, craft beer get together– but Lynch incisively focuses on the "social" part of investing. That is– people are not only attracted to stocks that *sound* interesting and are widely discussed in media (and Reddit subgroups), but also play well at social events. When attending a social function, and the discussion turns to investing, everyone wants to sound like they have a hot idea. Today, serving guests bourbon flights is more common than hosting "cocktail parties," but Lynch's investment principles are timeless.

1) IT SOUNDS DULL– OR EVEN BETTER, RIDICULOUS
2) IT DOES SOMETHING DULL
3) IT DOES SOMETHING DISAGREEABLE

These first three principles of Lynch's are really quite similar, and can be combined to form one of his main theses: that some of the best stocks often aren't well known. They also might sound strange and do unpopular things. Lynch discusses a company of his era with a really ridiculous name: Pep Boys– Manny, Moe, and Jack. An automotive service and repair chain (boring industry), with a name like the three stooges– anyone mentioning this one would really turn people off at the cocktail party. And of course, it was a great growth stock for nearly two decades. Another company Lynch mentions–Automatic Data Processing– sounds really generic. The largest payroll company for decades, it was a winner in Lynch's day and is still rewarding investors to this day with shares up nearly 40,000% from its IPO.

Lynch compares boring names like Automatic Data Processing (NYSE:ADP) to the fictitious "GeneSplice International." Wouldn't you rather talk about GeneSplice International to your friends? I think today's equivalent would be real corporate names like Riot Blockchain or FuelCell Energy. These SOUND exciting, but their long-term usefulness for the average investor is suspect. I always liked the name Jack Henry Associates (Nasdaq:JKHY). Can you imagine bringing that one up at a social get together? It sounds like a local insurance firm, not a provider of technology solutions with a $12 billion market cap. Oh– did I mention that the stock is up 47,000% since its IPO in 1986. Another modern ridiculous name is MongoDB. Whenever I read the name Mongo, I can't help but think of the character of Mongo in Mel Brooks' zany western comedy classic "Blazing Saddles." Mongo is a mute, illiterate outlaw who punches a horse unconscious. MongoDB (Nasdaq:MDB), however, is a database company taking on Oracle sporting a stock price up 15-fold since 2017.

Lynch declares your next great stock pick may have an absurd name or one that bores you to tears, and isn't in a sexy industry like today's hot ones: Blockchain, electric cars, and Artificial Intelligence.

4) IT'S A SPINOFF

Spinoffs occur when large corporations take a division and allow it to become independent as a separate publicly-traded company. The most famous spinoff occurred when AT&T "Ma Bell" was broken up and seven new regional "Baby Bell" companies were formed. According to research by Jim Osman of The Edge Group, and cited by *Kiplinger* magazine, spinoffs can be strong value plays as they are often under-followed by Wall Street and end up posting index-beating returns. One of my better performing stocks has been Match (Nasdaq:MTCH), an aggregation of dating sites such as Tinder, OKCupid, PlentyOfFish, and of course Match.com. Match was a wholly owned subsidiary of Interactive Corp. (Nasdaq:IAC), which itself is an agglomeration of internet properties. Shares of Match are up 120% from the date of the spinoff in July of 2020.

5) THE INSTITUTIONS DON'T OWN IT, AND THE ANALYSTS DON'T FOLLOW IT

How counterintuitive is this principle? Isn't it better to own stocks with a lot of buzz; the institutional darlings with BUY recommendations from the analysts? Absolutely not. You'll find time and again that when a company reaches the point where everyone is talking about it, it's probably time to get out completely; or at least consider taking some profits.

Let's consider Cisco in the Dot Com period. In 2000, Cisco was the most widely recommended stock on Wall Street, and by March 27th of 2000, Cisco's stock market capitalization reached $550 billion, making it the most valuable company on the planet. Time to get in? Think again. The stock soon cratered as the Dot Com bubble burst, and orphaned VC-backed startups were giving away their Cisco routers. There was no quick recovery, and even today– twenty-four years post the bubble– Cisco's market cap languishes hundreds of billions of dollars beneath its peak.

Another reason to avoid analyst recommendations is that research shows they are simply bad ideas. Burton Malkiel, in his classic *A Random Walk Down Wall Street,* cites a University of California study that reviewed the performance of the "strong buy" recommendations of Wall Street analysts. The study revealed that the analysts' "strong buy" recommendations *underperformed* the market as a whole by 3% per month. Perhaps more embarrassing, their SELL recommendations *outperformed* the markets by 3.8% per month. If there was ever a case for ignoring the professionals, this study supplied the evidence.

6) THE RUMORS ABOUND: IT'S INVOLVED WITH TOXIC WASTE AND/OR THE MAFIA

7) THERE'S SOMETHING DEPRESSING ABOUT IT

Let's consider these two principles "tongue and cheek" extensions of Lynch's theme espoused in principles 1-3, and 5; that a lack of sexiness often keeps potential competitors out of an industry segment, and likely makes the stocks more affordable. At the time of publication for this book, Artificial Intelligence companies– both privately-held and publicly-traded– are all the rage. Everyone wants to get into this business, and the valuations of these companies are sky high.

Certainly, we're not going to deliberately seek out companies with negative rumors swirling about them. In fact, negative rumors are a short seller's dream, and can cause stocks to plummet. However, Lynch uses this principle to discuss Waste Management, which of course disposes of garbage. And for many years– it was rumored that organized crime controlled a significant amount of garbage commerce in the Northeastern United States. Waste Management certainly doesn't sound sexy and picking up garbage even less attractive, but that didn't stop Waste Management shares from growing approximately 100-fold from its IPO in 1971 to the time of *One Up On Wall Street's* publication.

When I teach my courses, I also use Waste Management to pivot to my point of CEOs and leadership. As we discussed earlier with Robert Herjavec and his focus on the CEO, Waste Management was led by an extraordinary CEO in Wayne Huizenga. He started as a garbage collector himself, picking up trash with one truck in South Florida. Amazing companies are always built by amazing CEOs. And sometimes great companies– think Polaroid, IBM, Xerox, Blackberry– either disappear or become also-rans because of lackluster leadership.

Lynch illustrates his "depressing" Principle #7 with Service Corporation International. Besides having a dreadfully generic name, it's also in the funeral business. What could be a more depressing industry? No one wants to discuss owning a funeral stock at a cocktail party. But that's

Lynch's point– it's not the type of industry that attracts a lot of competition. Service Corporation stayed beneath Wall Street's radar screen for a long time, but by the late 1980s the stock was up 20-fold.

8) IT'S A NO-GROWTH INDUSTRY

Lynch doubles-down on cemetery and funeral operator Service Corporation when discussing No-Growth industries. Fast growing industries– like Artificial Intelligence– attract a lot of attention. I recently read an article in the *Boston Business Journal* in which a venture capitalist discussed the stampede into Artificial Intelligence: "Every investor pitch we see right now, entrepreneurs are trying to position their companies as AI companies." And as soon as you build something interesting in information technology, Venture Capitalists start pouring billions into startups to disrupt your success. Building cemeteries doesn't attract as much attention.

Another No-Growth industry I often discuss is railroads. No one is laying down more railroad track and there isn't a new railroad company getting funded by Venture Capitalists every week! The "Golden Age" of railroads began in 1865 and peaked in 1916. Yet look at the big players in the space: Norfolk Southern, CSX, and Union Pacific. These stocks are all up 10-15x over the last 20 years. In the same period, a once sexy stock like Cisco has only limped along, far below its peak nosebleed price set back in 2000.

9) IT'S GOT A NICHE

Lynch isolates possessing a niche as one of the most important attributes for successful companies. If a firm has a niche, it means it has a specialized place in the market; that its offering is unique and defensible. Lynch discusses the big city newspapers that once had strangleholds on daily print advertising. For most of 20th century America, the daily newspaper was a foundational component of a community. It's where you perused current events, scoured for jobs, researched stock quotes, and bought and sold merchandise in the classified section. Of course, the internet monumentally disrupted all of these information franchises. If you have a niche, you possess defensible walls that keep competitors out and customers in. NVIDIA currently has a niche in state-of-the art chips for processing AI. Niches may not last forever, but for a time be-ing– when exploited– they can become turbocharged engines of profit. We'll see the niche theme echoed when we discuss the concepts of "Toll Roads" and "Economic Moats."

10) PEOPLE HAVE TO KEEP BUYING IT

Wouldn't it be amazing if you owned a company and people were forced to buy the product? The FTC would frown on such a monopoly, but there are isolated pockets of industry that enjoy such a franchise. In the 1990s Genzyme (now a part of Sanofi) developed Ceredase, the first effective treatment for Gaucher's disease, a previously rare, untreatable and potentially fatal genetic disorder. At the time, Ceredase was the most expensive drug ever sold, costing on average $150,000 per patient per year. It's a moral question as to how a drug like Ceredase should be priced, but the Genzyme franchise on treating Gaucher's transformed the biotech into a billion-dollar revenue company. Along with pharma-ceuticals, Lynch discusses soft drinks, razor blades, and cigarettes as items that consumers must replenish, or are unfortunately addicted to. In the 1980s Warren Buffett famously stated: "I'll tell you why I like the cigarette business. It costs a penny to make. Sell it for a dollar. It's

---

addictive. And there's fantastic brand loyalty." According to *TIME* magazine, Marlboro branded cigarettes rank just behind the iPhone as the most profitable product sold. Beyond the moral questions as to whether one wants to be invested in the cigarette industry or own a company selling an expensive pharmaceutical, exists the exercise of analyzing *why* your prospective investment will be successful. Does the company have a product that is unique, beloved, and/or addictive?

11) IT'S A USER OF TECHNOLOGY

Technology is now so ubiquitous that this piece of advice may sound a little dated, much like Lynch's talk of the "cocktail party." Lynch suggests not investing in technology firms directly, but focusing on the firms that benefit from advancements in technology, like one of his favorites: Automatic Data Processing. It's an important point when one thinks of industries that might be disrupted by technology: newspapers, navigation devices, alarm clocks, musical records, etc. And then pivot to what industries could benefit from technology changes: discount brokerage, dating sites, travel, and more. I tend to think that if virtual reality headsets become commonplace, online dating could evolve from sending messages back and forth to an immersive experience. A date could exist in a virtual world where romantics might buy virtual gifts, and attend a virtual only event. Lynch and Buffett eschewed technology, which in their career heydays, was a more exotic industry to consider. Today's populace is fully immersed in technology, so avoiding the space isn't congruent with our tech-enabled existences. But the exercise of contemplating who gets hurt and helped by technological changes will be fruitful.

12) THE INSIDERS ARE BUYERS

Insider Buying occurs when company executives and directors purchase shares of their own company's stock on the open market. This should not be confused with exercising options, which generally involves buying stock at a discounted price. Insider Buying is often interpreted as a sign of confidence in the company's future prospects because insiders presumably have a deeper understanding of the business than the general public. Information on insider activity– not to be confused with Insider Trading as portrayed in the movie 'Wall Street"– is available at multiple internet sites. These insiders must file forms with the SEC indicating their intended activity.

I've always utilized Yahoo! Finance, where if you click on the "Holders" tab and then click on "Insider Roster," you can see a summary of recent insider activity. Click on "Insider Transactions" and you'll see detailed purchase activity for the most recent six months and sell activity for 24 months. Lynch writes he likes it when he sees several insiders buying as opposed to one. Be careful when utilizing this data as Insider Buying can be undertaken as a PR ploy. There have been cases where a CEO will announce they are making a large purchase of shares, and then never fully buy the targeted amount.

13) THE COMPANY IS BUYING BACK SHARES

A company can take its profits, buy its own shares, and then retire those bought shares. When a company buys shares, it's like removing a slice of pie. If I get one of eight slices of a pie, that's 12.5% of the pie. But if the pie is reduced to seven slices, my one slice represents 14.29% of the pie. This is good for shareholders, as their individual portion of the profits increases.

As Lynch points out, if a company bought back half their shares, they would double their earnings per share without actually increasing profits. Buffett generally prefers that companies eschew paying dividends with their excess capital, and instead buy back company stock. Be careful, however. Just as an announcement of an insider buying back stock can be utilized as a PR ploy, companies will issue press releases with their "intent" to buy back stock. This is generally perceived quite favorably and may provide a quick bump up for the stock. But the company isn't necessarily forced to buy back the intended figure.

That's it for Peter Lynch's thirteen principles for finding the "Perfect Stock," interpreted for modern times. Please do yourself a favor and read in full Lynch's *One Up On Wall Street*. You'll be 500% wiser after doing so, and hopefully your portfolio returns will increase by a commensurate figure.

The Downside of Peter Lynch's Magellan Fund

As extraordinary as Lynch's returns were during his tenure at Magellan, incredibly the average Magellan investor *lost* money while he was the portfolio manager. Even though the fund roared over thirteen years, posting average gains of 29%, the typical investor in the fund came out underwater. How could that be? INVESTOR BEHAVIOR– although this shouldn't be a surprise. The father of security analysis (and Warren Buffett's mentor) Benjamin Graham once said: "The investor's chief problem– and even his worst enemy– is likely to be himself."

Just as we articulated in Section 1 of this book– that most professional

---

investors don't hold their positions very long– most amateur investors don't hold their positions very long either. And according to a Fidelity Investments study, most Magellan holders entered the fund at a higher position than they exited. We can assume that the 1987 crash was a catalyst for many investors dumping their Magellan shares bought at much higher prices.

Even sadder than this Magellan fact, is that most equity investors experience returns *far beneath* the market averages. A study by Dalbar revealed that over 30 years, from 1987 to 2016, the typical equity fund holder (not manager) averaged a 3.98% return. In this same time period, the S&P 500 averaged 10.16% per year; and 1-year Treasuries averaged 3.99% per annum. Quantified in dollar figures, the typical investor who started the period with $100,000 in equity funds saw his/her holdings grow to $322,474. Yet an investor in the S&P saw his/her $100,000 grow to $1,822,711.

Imagine that! The typical equity fund holder experienced a return 1/6 of the S&P, and would have been better off just owning Treasuries. Once again, we ask– how can it be? The answer becomes obvious. If investors can't make money owning Magellan (which sported the greatest returns in the history of the mutual fund industry), they are going to have a really tough time making money holding the legions of high-cost, high-turnover, low-performing mutual funds that make up the rest of the pack.

I don't want you to get depressed. In fact, this sobering news should help you pivot to championing a long-term strategy of investing in the S&P 500 for many years and leaving the position alone. As I argued in Section II, put the bulk of your equity allocation in index funds. The money you utilize for individual stock picks should be a much smaller percentage (see page 174).

Warren Buffett: "The Oracle"

Frequently lauded as the greatest U.S. stock market investor of all-time, this superlative actually doesn't do Warren Buffett justice. Buffett isn't just one of the greatest investors of all time, he is one of the greatest businessmen of all time. It is often lost that Berkshire Hathaway is far more than a personal investment portfolio, but actually the 7th largest publicly-traded company in the U.S. by market capitalization and the 5th largest U.S. company by revenue ($364 billion in 2023). Berkshire is a colossal amalgamation of dozens of different companies– many wholly owned– and some partially. Over the decades, Buffett has supervised (with an underappreciated deftness) dozens of executives, who manage this quilt of operating divisions.

Just in case you don't know much about the 94-year-old Buffett, or need a refresher, he has been the CEO of Berkshire Hathaway (NY-SE:BRKA) since 1966. Buffett refashioned Berkshire from a Massachusetts-based textile producer into an Omaha, Nebraska based conglomerate with more than 60 wholly-owned companies (most with distinct brands). Among Berkshire's multitude of holdings are GEICO, Duracell, Dairy Queen, BNSF Railway, Lubrizol, Fruit of the Loom, Helzberg Diamonds, Long & Foster, FlightSafety International, Pampered Chef, BusinessWire, and NetJets.

Berkshire also owns 38.6% of Pilot Flying J; 26.7% of the Kraft Heinz Company; and significant minority holdings in American Express (17.6%), Wells Fargo (9.9%), The Coca-Cola Company (9.4%), Bank of America (6.8%), and Apple (5.22%).

Buffett doesn't believe in stock splits, so Berkshire shares currently trade at around $600,000. Buffett's 16.45% stake in the company puts his net worth at over $120 billion (the 10th richest in the world). In the 58 years since Buffett took control of Berkshire, the stock has delivered a compounded annual growth rate of 19.8%.

When I discuss Buffett in my investment classes, I always recommend Roger Lowenstein's biography *Making of an American Capitalist* for further reading, as it more fully captures Warren Buffett's career as a businessman, not just his wisdom and advice on stock picking (of which many other biographies solely focus).

As a stock picker, Buffett is known as a value investor, and was a disciple of Ben Graham (previously mentioned as the father of Securities Analysis). Buffett's recently deceased friend and Vice-Chair of Berkshire, Charlie Munger, is credited with helping steer Buffett away from strict value investing into more growth names. In the 1980s Buffett found some of his most successful investments moving towards companies like Coca-Cola and Gillette; names bought at reasonable prices but also growing earnings.

There are many books and articles written about Buffett and a deep examination of his career should be initiated by anyone seriously considering a profession (or significant avocation) as an investor. However, for the time constrained, here is an abbreviated look at what I consider to be the top seven precepts of the "Oracle of Omaha" that all investors should employ.

1) MAKE SURE YOU UNDERSTAND THE BUSINESS

I think this is the #1 commandment. If you buy a stock and have absolutely no idea what the company does, it's akin to swinging a bat with a blindfold on. You're just hoping to hit something. If you read an article recommending "10 Stocks for the Biden Era," or "Five Picks for the AI Revolution" and then invest in one of these names, BUT have never used the product or service, you are (as Gordon Gekko put it in the movie "Wall Street") "blind walking around without a cane." If you are successful with the stock, it's more luck than skill. If the stock drops 20% or meanders for six months (as they often do: see the section on "Stern's Laws"), you'll feel little gumption to hold the stock, and then sell at a loss. And buying high and selling low was never a good recipe for stock market success.

Buffett– who is a genius and likely capable of learning about any subject– focused on industries he knew very well. For many decades he eschewed technology companies even though he counted Microsoft's Bill Gates as one of his best friends. He picked up Apple shares only after the iPhone maker became more of a consumer-facing tech company. I've said it many times in the book, when you make an individual stock pick, make sure *you are the analyst* and can describe why you think the company will be successful; not because you read an article, but because your experience of the product or service compels you to feel its worth investing in.

2) BUY AT A VALUE PRICE

As a Ben Graham acolyte, Buffett initially focused his investments on companies with deeply discounted valuations. Graham's thesis was to buy companies whose market valuation was *lower* than the net Current

Assets. In Financial Accounting, the net Current Assets figure is derived by subtracting every debt a company has to pay in its current fiscal year from all of its Current Assets (its cash and anything that can be turned into cash in one year). This type of valuation would represent the counterweight to the "Nosebleed Valuation." It would allow an investor to potentially buy a company's stock at a price less than what the company could be immediately sold for (or liquidated). Graham's magnum opus *Security Analysis* was written in the doldrums of the Great Depression, when this type of depressed valuation was common.

Buffett began his career seeking these Graham-like stocks (fair businesses at a wonderful valuation), but later changed to a more growth mentality (wonderful businesses at a fair valuation). Whether seeking an extraordinarily cheap valuation, or a reasonable valuation, Buffett is focused on getting what he believes is a good price. As I've said before, you don't want to treat the stock market like a casino. It's not about rolling the dice and hoping you get a good pair of numbers. Companies can be analyzed, and an appropriate valuation determined. No one wants to overpay for their TV, car, or house– and you shouldn't do it with your investments (see page 79).

3) BUY COMPANIES WITH NICHES AND PRICING POWER

Peter Lynch articulated the powerful investment opportunities offered by companies with niches. A niche typically generates a condition where consumers or businesses must buy the product, or feel the product is vastly more compelling than other offerings. This concept is congruent with that of the "Toll Bridge" or the "Economic Moat," ideas we will soon explore. When a company has a niche, it has pricing power, which Buffett puts at the top of his list of important attributes: "The single-most

---

important decision in evaluating a business is pricing power. If you've got the power to raise prices without losing business to a competitor, you've got a very good business." In discussing Warren Buffett's perspective, blogger Samuel Jeffrey cogently summed up the composition of a niche: "They could stem from a strong brand (think Coca-Cola or Apple), proprietary technology (as with patents held by pharmaceutical companies), network effects (like the ones bolstering Facebook or Uber), cost advantages (enjoyed by large manufacturers with economies of scale), or even regulatory protections (like those surrounding utilities)."

Pfizer introduced Viagra in 1998 with patent protection in the U.S. through 2019, and worldwide through 2012. In its first quarter in 1998, the "little blue pill" generated $400 million in worldwide revenue. In its peak years, the ED medication was pulling in an average of $1.8 billion each year worldwide. Competition didn't surface until 2004 with the release of Levitra.

Put another way, you want to find "little blue pills"– products that people really want and need, and there is limited competition. Before buying any company always ask yourself– can this product be easily replicated? Can your prospective investment maintain pricing power? Does it have a unique property/business model/brand/patent that is difficult for other companies to assail?

4) AVOID COMPANIES REQUIRING SIGNIFICANT CAPITAL INVESTMENTS

Buffett advocates investors be highly discerning about the industries they consider. Some industries, like technology, are highly scalable. That is, they create intellectual property that is replicated or utilized with little increased cost. Microsoft bought an operating system from another

Seattle-based software company for $50,000, tinkered with the code, and then resold it as the brains for IBM's personal computer. Facebook and Google create a centralized software service that can be utilized by billions. Other industries such as Airline, Automobile, and Telecommunication respectively utilize immense amounts of capital to acquire, fuel and staff their jets; build massive factories and ship autos; and install and maintain thousands of miles of wires and cables to enable telephony and data transmission. Buffett's distaste for these capital intensive industries– particularly airlines– was concisely issued in his 2007 Berkshire Hathaway Annual Letter: "The worst sort of business is one that grows rapidly, requires significant capital to engender the growth, and then earns little or no money. Think airlines." In 2018, Buffett extolled the virtues of technology companies like Google and Apple: "The four largest companies today by market value do not need any net tangible assets. They are not like AT&T, GM, or Exxon Mobil, requiring lots of capital to produce earnings. We have become an asset-light economy." Companies that require a lot of machinery and physical assets to function are typically far less profitable than the asset-light businesses Buffett extols.

5) BUY FOR THE LONG TERM
Berkshire Hathaway often owns stocks for decades. What's extraordinary is that this simple discipline may be the most important ingredient of Buffett's success. While most portfolio managers are constantly moving in and out of their stock positions, getting excited about a 20% to 30% gain, Buffett isn't interested in selling unless there is some dramatic change in the business. If earnings are growing, and the capital commitments are low, he's happy. "Our favorite holding period is forever," Buffett wrote in one of his shareholder letters. "We are just the opposite

of those who hurry to sell and book profits when companies perform well but who tenaciously hang on to businesses that disappoint. Peter Lynch aptly likens such behavior to cutting the flowers and watering the weeds."

6) YOU DON'T NEED TO BE DIVERSIFIED

While this principle seems counterintuitive, interpret the concept as Buffett insisting an investor be laser focused on each investment opportunity. It's always a good idea to have multiple industries in one's portfolio, but you don't need 100 different stocks. Investors should instead think of making a limited number of investments– over their investing career– that are significantly researched and scrutinized. Buffett described this principle during a speech at Georgetown University: "You only have an opinion on a few things. In fact, I've told students if when they got out of school, they got a punch card with 20 punches on it, and that's all the investment decisions they got to make in their entire life, they would get very rich because they would think very hard about each one."

7) BE A CONTRARIAN

Buffett doesn't believe in following the crowd. If an investor buys stocks when the market is hitting new highs, IPOs are sprouting everyday, and it's easy to find companies trading at 30x sales with no profits– these are not the conditions when one should put new money to work. Heed Buffet's warning: "Most people get interested in stocks when everyone else is. The time to get interested is when no one else is. You can't buy what is popular and do well."

Conversely, when the market is down 20%, 30%, or even 40%; and there are no IPOs; and panic grips Wall Street– this is the time to invest. Buffett sums up this contrarian viewpoint perfectly: "Try to be fearful when others are greedy and greedy only when others are fearful." It isn't easy to do this– right? COVID really was scary. The 2008 Financial Crisis really was scary.

Buffett decreed in an October 2008 *New York Times* op-ed that even though the market had corrected 30%, he wasn't deterred from his long-term strategy. "I've been buying American stocks," he declared. "In short, bad news is an investor's best friend. It lets you buy a slice of America's future at a marked-down price."

Herbert Wertheim: The Billionaire You've Never Heard Of ($5.0B)

Okay, so we've discussed Warren Buffett and Peter Lynch, but you're still not a believer in long-term investing. You think that trying to get rich patiently is for wimps, and anyone with real *cajones* must build their wealth through exotic trading strategies.

Well, let's meet another investor who unlike Buffett and Lynch, is not a professional. In fact, he is an optometrist who has built a multi-billion dollar portfolio through a discipline of patient, long-term stock investing.

Herbert Wertheim, who was first outed as a billionaire by *Forbes* in 2019, owns hundreds of millions of dollars in stocks like Apple and Microsoft purchased decades ago during their IPOs. An $800 million-plus position in Heico (an airplane-parts manufacturer) dates to 1992. Additional holdings include Google, GE, BP, and Bank of America.

A successful optical inventor, Wertheim would be worth tens of millions of dollars from his firm's optical tints and lab equipment. However, it is what Wertheim did with his millions that made him a billionaire.

He bought stocks and held them long-term. A classic Fundamental Analyst, Wertheim spends hours studying the intellectual property (patent) positions of companies in which he's interested.

His strategy can be best described as a combination of Warren Buffett and Peter Lynch. "My goal is to buy and almost never sell," Wertheim proclaims. "I let it appreciate as much as it can and use the dividends to move forward." Contrast Wertheim's strategy with the trigger-happy professional mutual fund managers we discussed earlier, who jettison their positions every year.

The Microsoft shares Wertheim bought during the 1986 IPO, which have been paying dividends since 2003, are now worth hundreds of millions.

His 1.25 million shares of Apple, some purchased during its 1980 IPO, and some when the stock was languishing at $10 in the 1990s, are worth approximately $200 million.

Stewart Horejsi: Another Patient Billionaire ($3.4B)

Another billionaire you've probably never heard of– who also attained incredible wealth by owning a stock position for decades– is Stewart Horejsi (pronounced hor-ish).

Horejsi bought into Berkshire Hathaway– Warren Buffett's massive conglomerate– starting in 1980. He began buying stock in Berkshire for as little as $265.00 per share after reading John Train's *The Money Mas-*

ters, which features Warren Buffett along with other top investors of that era.

Now worth approximately $3 billion according to *Forbes*, Horejsi began attending Berkshire annual meetings when there were fewer than a dozen people sitting in folding chairs. Berkshire's annual meetings are now known as the "Woodstock for Capitalists," attracting thousands and commanding significant media attention.

Horejsi was initially prompted to invest in Berkshire due to competition he was facing with his family welding business. He started with 300 shares at prices ranging from $265 to $330, and gradually increased his stake to 5,800 shares at its peak. He began reducing his position in 1998, and now owns approximately 4,300 shares. As of this writing, Berkshire shares (BRKA) are trading at over $600,000.

The most important lesson to consider here is the tremendous discipline and patience Horejsi has displayed by holding Berkshire shares for so long– now standing at more than four decades. He stomached a significant decline in stocks in the early 1980s, a gut-wrenching stock market crash in 1987, a Bear market in 1990, the Dot Com bust, the 2008 Financial Crisis, and other hiccups and corrections along the way.

He didn't sell any shares until 1998, and still retains the majority of his position.

PART V

VALUATION BASICS

HOW DO WE DETERMINE VALUE? A conversation on stock valuation almost always starts with the P/E ratio: the price of the stock relative to its earnings per share (EPS). If this sounds confusing, there is an easy way to simplify it. Let's say you walk into a local restaurant that you enjoy and you ask the owner how much his sales are, and he replies $2 million annually. And you say: "Wonderful– may I ask you how much your profits are?" And he replies "$200 thousand annually." And you decide you want to buy the establishment and you offer him $3 million for the restaurant. That means you are offering him a price of 15:1 his profits; $3 million for his $200K in profits. So, we could say that you are offering to pay a P/E of 15 for the restaurant. If he counters and says he wants $4 million for the restaurant, that means he is asking for a P/E of 20; his $4 million ask is 20x the restaurant's annual profits of $200 thousand.

See– that was easy. However, understanding the P/E of a publicly traded company might be more confusing because investors commonly quote the value of a company on a per share basis. We typically don't speak of overall market valuation when we discuss stocks; we speak of

---

per share valuation. If I ask you, what's Apple trading at? You would probably respond with a quote of the share price: $194.43. You wouldn't say $3 trillion and 20 thousand dollars.

Additionally, in stock market vernacular, we often don't discuss the profits in total, we divide them by the number of shares and utilize an EPS figure: earnings per share.

Let's look at the example here:

Superlinear Electronics (a made-up name) earns $10 million in profits. And let's say that Superlinear Electronics has 10 million shares. $10 million in profits divided by 10 million shares equals $1.00 of profits per share.

Therefore Superlinear Electronics EPS = $1.00 per share. Profits and Earnings and Net Income are the same thing.

If Superlinear Electronics has a share price of $20.00, and it has EPS (profits per share) of $1.00, that means its P/E is 20.

P = Price of Stock $20.00
E = Earnings per share $1.00 EPS   PE=20

Here's another example. Let's say Epiphanous AI (also a made-up name) trades at $62.50 per share and has earnings per share (EPS) of $2.50. Let's add on that the company has 4 million shares of stock out-standing (in existence).

Take a look at the equation below, which offers a holistic view of PE combined with overall market valuation. If you can understand this, then you understand P/E!

25= P	= $250 mil. (market cap) /	4 mil. shares =	$62.50 per share	= P = 25
E	$10 mil. (earnings) /	4 mil. shares =	$2.50 EPS	E

A few things that are important to note, is that you can easily find the P/E quoted at sites like Google and Yahoo! Finance. So, if you're math averse you can utilize these sites. HOWEVER– caveat– sometimes these sites have incorrect data. So, you might want to practice calculating a P/E on your own. In order to get the most accurate data, go to the Investor Relations web link for a company you are considering investing in. Find a year-end earnings report, and look at the full-year EPS. Plug that EPS number into your P/E calculation.

Another important consideration, is that sometimes you'll hear folks on CNBC (or read articles) where investment professionals talk about *forward* earnings and forward P/E. The P/E that we've discussed heretofore is utilizing previously reported or Trailing Twelve Months (TTM) earnings. The Trailing Twelve Months P/E is the more traditional metric, as it compares actual reported earnings over the last twelve months.

The forward P/E incorporates an "E" that is based on what Wall Street analysts *think* a company will report. Be careful here, because if a company doesn't actually report numbers (E) in line with what optimistic analysts predict, and disappoints the Street, then the (P) stock price often tumbles.

What's a Good P/E?

Okay, so we can calculate a P/E or find it on Yahoo! Finance, but what does it mean if a company has a P/E of 20 or 30? Is that good, bad?

THE SHARK INVESTOR
VALUATION BASICS

Well, like a lot of things in life, there's never a simple answer. But we can start with looking at the average P/E of the S&P 500, which as of this writing, is 26.21. During the last fifteen years, with the exception of the "Great Recession," the P/E ratio of the S&P 500 has generally hovered around the average of 19.4x.

So, for a simple answer, if you're researching a stock that has a P/E of 15, you know that it is well below the current (and recent historical) average of the S&P 500. Conversely, if you see a company with a P/E of 65, you know that it's more than twice as high as the typical company in the S&P 500.

If it hasn't become apparent yet– theoretically, you want a low P/E! If you're going to buy a company, do you want to pay a lot for it, or a little? If you're buying a car, do you want to buy from the dealer with the lowest price or the highest price? If you're buying a house, would you prefer to pay below asking or above it?

Back to the previous example of a restaurant that you're considering buying, if the restaurant has $200 thousand in profits, would you like to pay $3 million for the restaurant at 15x earnings, or the proprietor's ask of $4 million (which is a P/E of 20)?

I think most of us would like to pay $3 million, and save the other $1 million. What we're looking for is a good value. Paying LESS for something is better than paying more.

Another way to think about P/E ratio is in terms of earnings yield. Let's explain: if you were to buy a company for $100 million and each year you pocketed $5 million in profits from the company, it means you paid a P/E of 20/1. And the $5 million in profits is 5% of your purchase price. So, think of the company as a CD. You invested $100 million and you're getting 5% back each year. That compares pretty well with most fixed income investments right now. However, if you paid $200 million for the same company with $5 million in profits, now you've got a P/E ratio of 40. And your earnings yield of 2.5% is well below a typical 1-year CD rate. On the surface, this is less attractive than getting the 5% yield.

When buyers are willing to pay more for something, we generally think that's it's WORTH paying more; that there is some quality about the offering that makes buyers want to increase their offers. And for publicly-traded companies, the quality of earnings is judged by the *growth* of the earnings. Are profits going up? Have they been going up? If profits have increased each of the last five years, and are expected to go up the next five years, then we might feel compelled to pay a higher price for the earnings.

That's exactly how it works in the stock market. Investors will pay higher P/Es when they believe that earnings are likely to grow in the future. Now you're ready for the PEG ratio.

PEG Ratio

The PEG ratio is used to determine a stock's value while taking the company's earnings growth into consideration, thus providing a more complete picture than the stand-alone P/E ratio.

A low P/E ratio may make a stock look like a good buy. However, if earnings have been declining, and they are not expected to grow, then a company deserves a low P/E ratio. Remember earnings alone are not what's important. It's the *future* earnings growth that Wall Street is more concerned about. The PEG ratio produces a number that takes this ever important metric into account.

In order to calculate the PEG Ratio, the P/E ratio is divided by its growth rate (which is a projected 5-year growth rate). Here are some examples:

Smith Distribution has a P/E of 25, and expected earnings growth rate of 25%:
25/25= PEG of 1
A company with a PEG of 1 would be considered fairly valued.

Schimmel Supplies has a P/E of 36, and expected earnings growth rate of 12%:
36/12= PEG of 3
A company with a PEG of 3 would be considered overvalued.

Wales Medical has a P/E of 25, and expected earnings growth rate of 50%:
25/50= PEG of .5
A company with a PEG of .5 would be considered undervalued.

A fast growing company with a PEG of 1 or below is great. A PEG of 3 is high. A PEG of 1.5 is a decent value for very popular/ fast growing companies at the peak of their growth cycles.

Notice that in the world of integers, we haven't moved very far: 1, 2, 3. But in the world of PEG, the difference between 1 and 3 is monumental.

The Real Estate Analogy

Thinking about P/E and PEG ratios is analogous to how people think about valuing real estate.

When someone looks at a home and is trying to determine value, they often consider price per square foot. If you are paying $1 million dollars for a home, are you buying a 5,000 sq. foot home, a 2,500 sq. foot home, or a 1,000 sq. foot home.

The PEG Ratio is analogous to the key metrics you would use for determining the right value for a home. If I tell you a home costs $1 million, what are your first two questions to help you determine if it's a good price?

For a company, it doesn't matter that much how many factories it has, how many employees it has, or how much intellectual property it has. What matters is the size of the profits that those factories, employees, and patents can produce. If they can't produce profits, then all of those assets may not be worth that much.

A company's profits are akin to a home's square footage.

So, if I tell you that I've got a home that's $1 million and has 2,000 square feet, what's the next question you should ask? What is the qualitative piece of information that might determine if you'll consider this home?

Location, Location, Location. *Where* is the home? Is it in Wellesley, MA; Los Altos, CA; or Highland Park, TX– all affluent suburbs. Or, is it in a depressed mill town 200 miles from a major city?

Learning about location is the qualitative equivalent to determining earnings growth in a company. With these three pieces of information: price, earnings, and earnings growth rate, we can get a decent idea if we are paying a fair price for a company.

Profit Margin: How Easily Are Profits Created

Another important metric to consider is Profit Margin, a calculation of the percentage of total revenue that becomes profits. You can easily find this figure at online finance sites like Yahoo! and Google, but its not too difficult to calculate yourself.

Let's look at the example below for DEF company. The firm has $1.5 billion in total sales, and $1.25 billion in costs. That leaves DEF with $250 million in profits.

If we divide the $250 million in profits by the total revenue of $1.5 billion, we'll get 16.66%.

　　　$1.50 Billion in Sales
- 　 $1.25 Billion in Costs
= 　 $250 Million in Profit

$250 Million
$1.5 Billion　　　=16.66% Profit Margin

A Profit Margin of 16.66% is actually pretty healthy. A report issued by New York University's Stern School of Business revealed the average net Profit Margin is 7.71% across different industries. A simple rule of thumb is to think of 5% as a low margin, 10% as a healthy margin, and 20% a high margin.

In fact, if you're researching a company and see that it has a Profit Margin of 20% or higher, get excited! And unless there are specific circumstances to consider otherwise, I generally avoid companies with Profit Margins below 5%.

Remember, increasing profits drive stock prices. And companies with high Profit Margins have the capital to invest, pay dividends, buy back stock, or pay bonuses to employees. In 2019, *Barron's* took a look at the returns of companies with the highest Profit Margins, to see if simply investing in those stocks was a valid investment strategy.

The 10 most-profitable firms in the S&P 500, based on 2019 margins, were: VeriSign (VRSN), Visa (V), CME Group (CME), Mastercard (MA), Broadcom (AVGO), Alexion Pharmaceuticals (ALXN), Vertex Pharmaceuticals (VRTX), CBOE Global Markets (CBOE), Regeneron Pharmaceuticals (REGN), and Public Storage (PSA).

Barron's determined that this top 10 group had an average net Profit Margin of about 46%, and shares returned about 16% a year on average over the past three years. The average net Profit Margin in 2019 for S&P 500 companies was about 14%. The average stock in the S&P 500 had returned about 8.5% over the same span. Thus, the firms with the highest Profit Margins delivered returns nearly double the S&P!

Price to Sales Ratio

The Price to Sales ratio is another excellent metric to consider when valuing stocks, particularly when there are no earnings. When there are earnings, you can utilize the P/E and PEG ratios, as well as Profit Margin.

But if there are no earnings, those three metrics won't do you much good.

You can, however, consider the value of the company relative to its sales. As an example, if a company has a total of $1 billion in sales, and its market valuation is $10 billion, then we would say it has a 10:1 (or 10x) Price to Sales ratio. If the market cap was $5 billion, then we would say it has a 5:1 Price to Sales ratio.

$5 Billion Market Cap   =   **5**
$1 Billion Sales (Revenue)   1

Of course, this begs the question, what's a *good* Price to Sales ratio. First, let's consider that the average Price to Sales ratio of the S&P 500 is around 2.5x. With that simple piece of information, we can start to determine if a company we're considering investing in has a low valuation or a high valuation.

Let's consider Snowflake (Nasdaq:SNOW), a high-flying software company throughout the 2021 COVID stock boom. By late October of 2021, Snowflake had a Price to Sales ratio exceeding 100. At face value, a Price to Sales ratio that is 40x higher than the typical company in the S&P, should be a valuation red flag. In fact, whenever you encounter a company with a Price to Sales ratio of more than 20x, you should take notice and proceed with caution. We'll spend more time on this subject when we get to our chapter on "Nosebleed Valuations."

On the other end of the spectrum, what if we come across ABC Software company (which I'm making up for this exercise) with no profits, and a Price to Sales ratio of 5x. Is this company worth buying?

A useful exercise is to extrapolate what the profit picture might look like when the company actually is in the black. That might provide an idea as to whether currently unprofitable ABC Software has an acceptable valuation.

Software is among the industries with the highest Profit Margins (Regional Banks surprisingly have the highest), with 20% being a common figure. So, if I go back to my unprofitable ABC Software company with sales of $1 billion, let's determine if sales are growing and at what pace?

Let's theorize that when the company hits $2 billion in sales, the firm is profitable and is sporting those industry-common 20% profit margins. Then we'll likely see ABC with earnings of $400 million. Now that I've developed a model for projected profits, I could go ahead and apply a future theoretical PE ratio to ABC Software. If ABC Software is projected to grow sales and earnings at 25% per annum, maybe we'll see a Price Earnings ratio of 30. So, if ABC Software at some point produces $400 million in profits, and trades at a PE of 30, then its valuation will be $12 billion.

And if I can buy ABC Software today– currently unprofitable with $1 billion in sales and a 5x Price to Sales ratio ($5 billion market cap); then I've got a good shot at making money with this company as earnings grow.

I'm illustrating this point because companies without profits often possess valuations that are depressed relative to a profitable peer. There are investors who will not touch unprofitable firms. See more at "Be Willing to Buy Unprofitable Companies."

Avoid Companies with Loads of Debt

Whenever you hear that a company has gone bankrupt, guess who gets to take over the assets? It's not the stockholders, it's the debt holders.

For those of us who have experienced financial friction in our lives, what's typically the genesis of it? It's the mortgage or rent we have to pay; the car loan, the student loan, and the credit card debt.

For companies, it's the same issue on a much larger scale. Companies might have millions and even billions in debt. It's okay to have debt, but how much? Here are two handy ratios to keep in mind. When you're investigating your prospective stock picks, make sure you take a look at the Current Ratio and the Debt to Equity Ratio.

CURRENT RATIO

The current ratio is a financial metric that assesses a company's ability to meet its short-term obligations, also known as liquidity. It's calculated by dividing a company's Current Assets by its Current Liabilities. Here's a breakdown of the definition.

Current Assets: These are assets that a company can convert into cash within one year. This typically includes cash, inventory, and accounts receivable.

Current Liabilities: These are debts that a company owes and expects to pay within one year. This includes accounts payable, short-term loans, and accrued expenses.

By comparing these two values, the Current Ratio indicates whether a company has enough readily available resources (Current Assets) to cover its upcoming financial commitments (Current Liabilities).

Essentially, a higher Current Ratio suggests a greater capacity to pay off short-term debts. However, what constitutes a "good" Current Ratio can vary depending on the industry. Generally, a ratio of 2:1 is considered very healthy, although some industries may function well with a lower ratio.

Current Assets	=	$550 million	= 2	Current Ratio
Current Liabilities		$225 million	1	

DEBT TO EQUITY RATIO

The Debt to Equity Ratio is a financial metric used to assess the proportion of a company's financing that comes from debt compared to equity. It is calculated by dividing a company's total liabilities (debt) by its shareholders' equity.

Total liabilities include all debts and obligations owed by the company, such as loans and bonds, while shareholders' equity represents the portion of the company's assets that belong to the shareholders, typically consisting of retained earnings and contributed capital.

A high Debt to Equity Ratio indicates that a company is primarily financed by debt, which can lead to higher financial risk due to increased interest payments and potential difficulty in servicing debt obligations.

Conversely, a low Debt to Equity Ratio suggests that a company relies more on equity financing (such as retained profits), which may indicate a stronger financial position and lower risk.

The optimal Debt to Equity Ratio varies by industry and company, and what is considered a "good" ratio depends on factors such as the company's growth prospects and profitability.

However, to be on the safe side, I would target companies that have Debt to Equity Ratios of 25% or less. And anything above 50% I would see as a red flag.

Total Debt	=	$1.2 billion	= 25%	Debt to Equity Ratio
Total Equity		$4.8 billion		

Reading financial statements and becoming conversant in a multitude of valuation metrics is what Equity Analysts do for a living. Many of them hold the CFA (Chartered Financial Analyst) designation, which is attained only through rigorous examination.

Don't despair if you haven't attained CFA status. Finding these two ratios on Yahoo! Finance, and staying within the suggested parameters, can act as a significant safety check.

Where Do I Find This Data? Yahoo! Finance

After reading Lynch's *One Up On Wall Street* in 1989, I was inspired to try my hand at stock analysis. There was no internet, so in order to find information about publicly traded companies one had to either call the Investor Relations department at a prospective company and ask them to mail out the firm's Annual Report and 10-K (similar to an Annual Report but filed with the SEC), or you could trot to a major library and seek out *Value Line* reports.

I'll never forget traveling to downtown Boston to the Kirstein Business Library and rummaging through reports on different companies I was considering investing in. Fortunately, *your* "library trip" can be to Yahoo! Finance, which I still consider to be the best source for free, easy-to-access, stock market information.

Whether you're scouting for P/E, PEG, Market Cap, Earnings Growth, Revenue Growth, Profit Margin, Current Ratio, Debt to Equity Ratio, or Insider Ownership– all the data is a click or two away.

To find most of this information, just plug in a stock symbol, or type in the company name in the window that reads "Search for news, symbols or companies." The "Statistics" tab will then provide all the fundamental data we have discussed in this book.

This is just a start. Yahoo! Finance has detailed information on company news, analysts' estimates, and financial statements. By spending time on Yahoo! Finance, an amateur investor will discover much of the data they will need to help make decisions. And truth be told– I once walked in on the CEO of a publicly-traded, billion-dollar revenue IT company checking his firm's stock price on Yahoo! Finance.

Stock Screener

A useful tool in getting your brain calibrated for stock picking is employing the Stock Screener at Yahoo! Finance.

With the Screener, you can input the criteria you're searching for in a stock– like a PE range and Profit Margin– and get a list of companies that meet your parameters.

Start at Yahoo! Finance, go to "Research," and click "Screeners." There are some interesting pre-built Screeners such as "Aggressive Small Cap Stocks" and "Undervalued Growth Stocks." You can click on "Create New Screener," and there are a number of filters you can utilize to uncover equities with a combination of the attributes you deem important.

You can build multiple screens and give them nicknames. I have a screener with filters for PE, PEG, 1-year change in revenue growth, and 1-year change in EPS. For my screener I chose companies with a PE of less than 50, a PEG no greater than 2, revenue growth exceeding 25%, and EPS growth above 25%.

254 companies (including foreign) actually meet these fairly stringent criteria, and most of them I've never heard of. The ones I've never heard of, I'll likely ignore. Remember– make your very first criterion of stock picking a company that you *know and understand* and love its products. Interestingly, Progressive Insurance and Booking Holdings (formerly Priceline) are the #2 and #3 companies listed. These companies I know– I've been a customer of both, and have used competitor products. This is where the screener becomes useful– pointing me in the direction of companies that I might never have thought of. And now I know they are fast growing, publicly-traded companies that are reasonably valued.

There are additional filters available for balance sheet metrics, ESG scores, volume, price movement, and more. Balance Sheet metrics such as Current Ratio, and Debt as percentage of Equity, are also critical for finding not just fast growing companies, but ones with healthy balance sheets as well.

PART VI

DO THIS AND FORGET ABOUT THAT

D O YOUR HOMEWORK OR "DUE DILIGENCE." Performing "due diligence" means researching prospective investments. Would you consider buying a car before you drove it? Of course not– you would visit three dealerships and compare prices. You would read about the car in *Consumer Reports*. You might buttonhole a driver of the prospective car and pepper them with questions on their experience and opinion of the vehicle.

How about a new TV? Would you just go into a store and buy any TV? You'd probably insist on reading reviews, and go to 2-3 different retailers and compare prices– correct?

But how many investors drop 5K or 10K on a stock on which they have done zero research? Unfortunately, I would say many investors buy stocks based on tips, online posts, magazine articles, etc.

Imagine that– a consumer will do significant research on a 1K television they're considering, but will make a 10K stock investment based on an online Meme!

A "Shark" investor will engage in a substantial amount of due diligence– or at least as much as you would when buying a car. You'll want to consider various qualities of the business, perform Top-Down analysis, perform Fundamental Analysis, and learn about the CEO.

Make sure you go through the stock picker's checklist on page 147 before you invest.

Forget About Getting Rich Quickly

As Warren Buffett once said (and I'm paraphrasing a bit), "It's a very powerful instinct to try and get rich quickly, but for the life of me, I can't

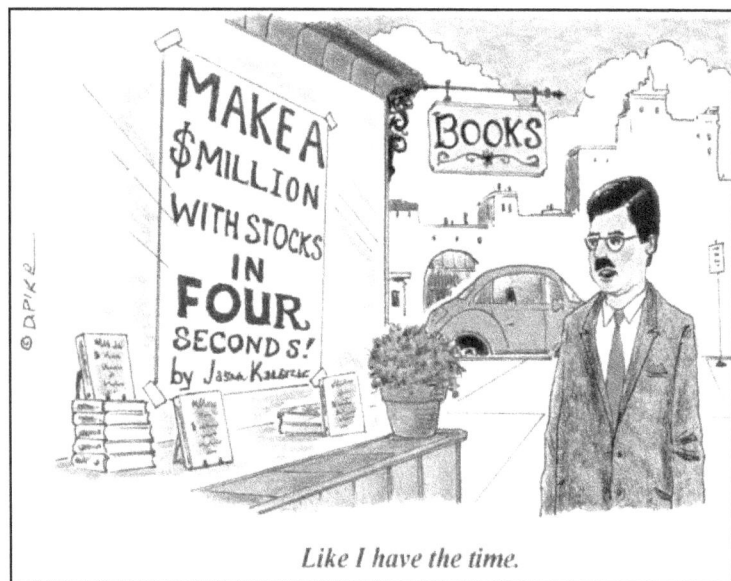

Like I have the time.

figure out how to do it." The "Oracle of Omaha" said it well: everyone wants to get rich, and people sure would love to get rich overnight.

How many of the books you see in a bookstore investment section are focused on strategies that claim to create instant wealth? How many of the ads you see on CNBC, and the ads you read in personal finance magazines, are methods, strategies, and schemes to make money rapidly? And easily, to boot!

And if they worked, wouldn't we all employ these strategies, retire– and enjoy lives golfing, yachting, and sipping wine?

Some people like to think of the stock market as a casino; something akin to picking the right number on a Roulette wheel.

There might be a few folks who get lucky here and there; but getting rich quickly is impossible for most.

Don't be seduced by get rich quick classes, books, and investment strategies.

Focus on getting rich slowly through patient investing.

Buy Companies You Do Business With and See Others Using the Product

WATERHOUSE My first multi-bagger, winning stock pick was buying shares in a discount brokerage firm called Waterhouse Securities. Waterhouse was known as a deep discount broker and competed against other discounters like Charles Schwab, Fidelity, and the now defunct Quick & Reilly. Waterhouse was acquired in 1996 by Toronto Dominion Bank (TD), and is a predecessor company to TD Ameritrade, which of course is now a part of Schwab. But back in 1991 I was a young stock market buck, and had made a few trades using the Waterhouse platform. At that time a $5,000 trade with a full-service firm like Merrill Lynch would cost about $200.00. Charles Schwab was priced at approximately $75.00, and Waterhouse would handle the same trade for around $35.00. After having made those initial trades with Waterhouse, I then learned it was a publicly-traded company. My positive experience as a customer sparked my investment interest, and I investigated the fundamentals of the firm.

Everything looked promising. The company had grown substantially during the 1980s, and continued to add offices even after the 1987 crash. The CEO, Larry Waterhouse, was the namesake founder and largest shareholder. These were elements of the company anyone could discern, but as a customer, I was privy to learning that Waterhouse's customer service was terrific. This was of course pre-internet, and you needed to call your broker to place a trade. Calls were promptly answered by polite and knowledgeable Waterhouse representatives. The transaction price was phenomenal with commissions well underneath the competition, and Waterhouse even offered a 10% discount on trades to their shareholders! This was a no-brainer!

I bought Waterhouse stock shortly after the 1991 Bull market began, and incredibly Waterhouse Securities finished 1991 as one of the best performing securities on the Nasdaq. It was my first multi-bagger winning stock pick.

YAHOO! 1996 was the first year I began actively using the internet, and I spent considerable time using the #1 search engine at the time: Yahoo! So, you need to think back to an era before Google. The internet was uncharted, and the best guide to finding relevant web sites was Yahoo!. It may be hard to imagine, but there were multiple search engines at this point of the internet's development such as Lycos, Alta Vista, Excite, Infoseek, Northern Light, and even one called Ask Jeeves. By late 1996, there was no question that the leader in the space was Yahoo! I used it constantly and could look around at my work colleagues and see it on their screens as well. Yes– these were the glorious early days of the internet before the Dot Com bubble, and it wasn't difficult to imagine a company like Yahoo! growing to a size 10x its 1996 status. My thinking was that simple. Even though the company had just recently become profitable, I figured in 10 years Yahoo's market cap would increase 10x as use of the internet proliferated. I ended up being very wrong. Instead of growing 10x in 10 years, Yahoo!'s share price went up 100x in four years!

PANERA BREAD I'll never forget the first time I dined at a Panera Bread restaurant in suburban Boston. My immediate impression was McDonald's crossed with Starbucks; more specifically the fast-food aspect of McDonald's mixed with the more sophisticated feel of Starbucks. I remember the delicious Moroccan Lentil soup I ate paired with Panera's scrumptious baguette, all the while sitting next to a fireplace. This was 2002 and definitely a new experience in the realm of fast-casual dining. I visited a couple of other Paneras and was impressed with the unique décor in each location, and the lines of customers. When I researched the stock, it had all of the elements I was looking for except it seemed a bit overvalued. I didn't want to pull the trigger at a PEG level that exceeded 1.5, and kept my powder dry. I didn't have to wait too long. As the drumbeat of an impending Iraq war became louder and louder, the stock market fell lower and lower. Eventually Panera reached a PEG of 1 and

I pounced. Shares moved up rapidly once the Iraq war looked highly winnable, and the stock was a multi-bagger winner.

BOSTON BEER One summer my wife was in a softball league and many of her teammates would quench their thirsts by swilling down Truly Hard Seltzer. Turns out Truly was a division of Boston Beer, whose flagship product was Sam Adams. I bought the stock, and Truly helped propel Boston Beer 3x from 2019 to 2021.

Other winning stocks that came directly from my experience as a customer have been: Chipotle, Visa, Netflix, Google, Crocs, Apple, and Facebook. These are all companies where I bought the products or used the service, and could make decisions based on *my experience*. For beginning investors, I might put this criterion at the top of the list. Before you make a stock pick, ask yourself– am I doing business with this company? What's so great about it? Can you delineate what makes it special and why you are using the product or service? If you're excited about a product, then go investigate if it might be a good stock.

Know Your CEO

Just as the "Shark Tank" investors pay very close attention to the entrepreneur presenting the business opportunity, stock market investors should look very closely at the CEOs of the publicly-traded companies in which they invest.

Venture Capitalists get rich by betting on an entrepreneur, and then riding their coattails of success. Think of the great fortunes built for Venture Capitalists who bet on Sergey Brin and Larry Page of Google,

Jeff Bezos of Amazon, and Mark Zuckerberg of Facebook. Yes– they are billionaires today, but they were once hungry, bootstrapping entrepreneurs groveling for capital.

We largely think of Google, Amazon, and Facebook as gargantuan publicly-traded companies, forgetting that they were once fledgling startups created by inexperienced entrepreneurs.

Many of the great stocks of the last 50 years were founder led companies– Bill Gates of Microsoft, Larry Ellison of Oracle, Philip Knight of Nike, Steve Jobs of Apple. They were founders who led their companies for multiple decades. The companies were their babies. They personally owned sizable blocks of the company's shares and they had a vested interest in seeing the companies prosper.

When you are considering investing in an individual security– know your CEO.

HOW TO SPOT A SUPERSTAR CEO

One of the great Venture Capital and public market investors of the last 30 years is Japanese businessman Masayoshi "Masa" Son– the CEO of Softbank. Masa and Softbank have been behind some of the most successful companies of the last few decades: Yahoo!, Uber, DoorDash, TikTok parent ByteDance, and Alibaba. Alibaba is probably Masa's most spectacular investment. The $20 million seed funding Masa provided is now worth over $140 billion.

Alibaba is one of China's publicly traded tech titans. When Masa met Alibaba's founder Jack Ma, he quickly knew he had found a superstar CEO. After a five-minute pitch from Jack Ma, Masa was ready to pull the trigger and make the $20 million dollar investment. What convinced Masa to invest in Alibaba? It was something he detected in his interac-

DO THIS AND FORGET ABOUT THAT

tion with Ma: "It was the look in his eye, it was an 'animal smell.'"

You may not be able to meet the CEO of a prospective company face-to-face and determine whether they possess a powerful "animal scent," but you might have a good shot at finding an interview with them on CNBC, a podcast, a YouTube appearance, or some other on-line media. What do they sound like to you? What ambitions and ideas do they articulate? Find out how much stock they own? Find out if they are a founder or handpicked by the founder?

Just recently, on a single episode of "Mad Money," CNBC's Jim Cramer hosted Broadcom's CEO Hock Tan, E.L.F Beauty's Tarang Amin, and ARM's Rene Haas. Cramer engaged in deeply penetrating interviews about these companies and their industry prospects allow-ing the viewer to get a feel for the CEO's passion and mastery of the details of their businesses.

Additionally, you can learn about a CEO's background by Googling around a bit. See if you can find a *Fortune*, *Forbes*, or *Business Insider* article that discusses the background of the executive. These media are essential for performing due diligence on companies and the execu-tives that lead them.

Buy Stocks with Founder/CEOs

One of the additional benefits of investing in companies with entre-preneurial Founder/CEOs, is that these leaders often pay themselves a lot less than hired hands. Because they own substantial amounts of shares in the company, they ask for salaries that are often a pittance relative to the non-founder, professional managers.

104   **Part VI**

Remember, if you're the founder, the company is *your* baby. You are often the largest shareholder, so there is nothing you want more than to see the stock price go up. Low executive pay is of great benefit to the shareholders, whereas huge salaries eat up profits and giant stock awards are dilutive to shareholders.

As an example, let's look at Niraj Shah, the CEO and Co-Founder of home furnishings company Wayfair (NYSE:W). Shah Co-Founded Wayfair with his college buddy Steve Conine, and Shah owns approximately 10% of the stock. With shares trading around $50.00 and a market value of around $6 billion, that means Shah is worth around $600 million. This figure is down from Wayfair's COVID peak when shares traded north of $300.00 and Shah was worth nearly $4 billion.

In any case, Shah is loaded! He doesn't need to draw a huge salary from Wayfair, and pays himself a paltry $80,000 salary with no bonuses or stock awards.

Compare Shah and his compensation to the typical non-founder CEO, who often asks for a monster pay package of big salary, outlandish bonuses, dilutive options, and a horrific golden parachute (meaning if he/she gets fired, they get a huge severance). Salaries are expenses, expenses depress earnings, and depressed earnings depress stock prices.

According to *Inc. Magazine* and *Fast Company*, a study revealed nearly half of 500 CEO founders surveyed paid themselves less than $100,000 a year, with 5 percent taking no salary at all!

Founders also dominate a *Fast Company* list of the 15 most fairly paid CEOs. The article compares CEO pay relative to the median pay of their employees. Eleven of the fifteen executives on the list are Founders or Co-Founders of their businesses.

While CEO compensation at S&P 500 companies averaged $16.7 million in 2022, founders of companies often pay themselves a lot less. It cannot be emphasized enough: Founder/CEOs are often your best investment.

Buy a "Toll Road"

The "Toll Road" is a favorite investment metaphor for Warren Buffett. The idea is that you have a business product or service so valuable, so unique, and so necessary that buyers must utilize it. Actual Toll Bridges or Toll Roads often serve as necessary (and perhaps unavoidable) connectors between two points. This is a critical concept to consider when analyzing prospective investments. It's desirable to invest in a company whose business offering is a must consumption.

In fact, Buffett the master investor, went one step further than most—he actually bought a Toll Road. In the late 1970s, Buffett bought 25% of the shares of the Detroit International Bridge Company, which owned the Ambassador bridge, the only bridge connecting Detroit with Windsor, Ontario.

As of today, the Ambassador is still the only bridge connecting Detroit and Canada, and is the busiest U.S.-Canadian border crossing, carrying 25% of all trade between the two coun-

tries. The bridge is still in private hands generating at least $60 million in annual revenues.

An article by Steve Chen published at *GuruFocus.com* eloquently describes the alluring attributes of a Toll Bridge: "A Toll Bridge possesses several favorable characteristics to shareholders: e.g., a monopoly-like market position, durable pricing power and predictable recurring cash streams. All these are attributable to the fact (or assumption) that there are very few alternative routes to compete with the bridge loaded with heavy traffic."

What are some Toll Roads today? I've been a long-term investor in both Visa and MasterCard. I've had different businesses over the years where I've taken customer credit card payments. When I first saw the 2.99% that the credit card companies were taking from my gross sales (right off of the top), I felt infuriated. The anger then transitioned to awe, as I realized the massive number of businesses that receive the majority of their sales via credit card purchases, with MasterCard and Visa taking a percentage of EVERY transaction. If you can't beat 'em, join 'em. I decided to become an investor in Visa, and then MasterCard. These could be the greatest Toll Roads in existence. They have virtually no meaningful competition and essentially act as tax on consumer GDP. Yes, there are American Express and Discover as minor competitors in credit. But the entire debit infrastructure is built on the networks of MasterCard and Visa. Imagine taking a small slice of every swipe! Visa's 2023 profit margin was in excess of 56%.

For twenty years Google has operated a Toll Road in internet search, generating 88% of the firm's $74 billion profit in 2023. Apple operates a Toll Road with its App Store. If you want to be a developer on the platform, you pay a fee every year. According to a CNBC analysis, the

App Store generated $85 billion of revenue in 2022. And it appears that NVIDIA has established (for the time being) a Toll Road in high-end chips for processing Artificial Intelligence applications. As Josh Brown, a CNBC commentator, pointed out recently: NVIDIA's Artificial Intelligence chips are just a starting point. Once you buy the chips you are locked into an ecosystem of NVIDIA software and services.

Contemplate the Evolution of the Company

Contemplate the evolution of a prospective investment. Fast growing companies are rarely complacent. What new markets can they attack?

After Venture Capitalist John Doerr invested in Amazon, he toured around Fry's Home Electronics (a now defunct retailer) with Jeff Bezos. At inception, Amazon was a retailer of books, and was competing against brick-and-mortar booksellers. Doerr recalled that as the duo walked through Fry's aisles, they realized Amazon could sell any of the products that were being sold at Fry's. For Doerr it was an epiphanous moment as he grasped that Amazon could become the "Everything Store."

Amazon eventually did begin to sell nearly everything. They also created the Prime membership. Later Amazon developed their giant cash cow in Amazon Web Services, and eventually bought Whole Foods making a foray into the $750 billion grocery market.

Talented and visionary CEOs can lead companies from being single product firms to competing in different channels. Microsoft's origins lie in developing an operating system for the first personal computer. They later expanded into multiple software lines, developed the X-Box, and acquired Linkedin and GitHub.

Google started with a search engine and later bought YouTube, Nest, and Android; and currently is making inroads into autonomous driving (with its Waymo unit).

CEOs are paid to grow the businesses. You should contemplate the expansion opportunities of a prospective investment. What new markets can it enter with its brand equity? What are natural extensions? If you're looking to hit a home run with your investment, it will need to be in a company with a long runway of product expansion (and/or acquisitions) ahead of it.

Invest Like a Founder/CEO

It's not just Warren Buffett or Herbert Wertheim or Stewart Horejsi who will own a company's stock for a long period of time. Guess who else will maintain an investment for decades? The Founder/CEOs of companies– they will own their own stock for multiple decades.

After Amazon went public, did Jeff Bezos sell all or most of his Amazon shares and buy the S&P 500? Did he feel he should diversify away from Amazon? Did Bill Gates rapidly sell his Microsoft stock after the firm's 1986 IPO and buy the S&P?

Absolutely not. These entrepreneurs held onto their stock for decades. That's how they became fabulously wealthy, and that's how you should think of your stock picking. You're not just picking some random company and hoping it goes up. You're investing in an entrepreneur– a visionary– just like the "Sharks" on "Shark Tank," and just like professional venture capitalists.

Did Larry Ellison (Oracle), Mark Zuckerberg (Facebook), Sergey Brin and Larry Page (Google Guys), Michael Dell, or Phillip Knight (Nike) sell their stock holdings and buy the S&P?

No, they kept the bulk of their wealth in the companies they founded. It's important to note I am not recommending you put the bulk of your equity allocation in individual stocks, rather a minor portion.

However, when we do buy individual stocks, we are going to seek out companies run by transformative entrepreneurs, and we are going to maintain our investments for significant periods of time.

We are not looking for short-term profit gains. Even doubling our money will be a lesser goal. A "Shark Investor" will hold his/her investments for extended periods of time: 5, 10, 15, 20, 25 years. Not 12 months.

Remember– the S&P 500 index never sells. The QQQ Nasdaq 100 ETF (see page 191) never sells (except when the stocks these funds track don't meet the index criteria).

Buy "Category Killers"

The term category killer was historically used in retail, but can be extended to refer to any company that dominates a niche– whether retail or a new technology. Companies that are category killers– as the name suggests– often put incumbent competitors out of business.

Toys R' Us was the category killer in toys for decades (until Walmart and Target usurped their position). Best Buy is the bricks and mortar category killer in electronics. Staples and OfficeDepot are the category killers in retail office supply. Home Depot and Lowe's dominate retail home improvement.

When you find these category killers early, you typically have an appreciating stock. An investment in any of the aforementioned names at their IPO prices would have been successful for several years.

But of course, you've got to be aware of what we'll talk about soon– disruption. It's hard to lock up a market forever. Just as a company like Toys R' Us disrupted the retail toy industry with their massive big box stores, they were disrupted by even bigger, big-box discount retailers, who sold the most popular toys at prices Toys R' Us couldn't match.

Investors once thought of IBM as the unassailable leader in computer technology. Some theorize IBM was nicknamed "Big Blue" because it was considered the bluest of the Blue Chip U.S. stocks. And of course today, "Big Blue" is pretty much considered an also-ran in many of the information technology segments it once dominated.

Who are some of the category killers today? Google crushes its competitors in web search. Netflix leads in streaming video. Dick's destroys in sporting goods. If you can find a category killer, you've probably increased your odds for owning a winning stock.

THE SHARK INVESTOR
DO THIS AND FORGET ABOUT THAT

Buy Disruptors

The term "Disrupt" is used frequently in the world of Venture Capital and entrepreneurship. Venture Capitalists look for companies that can upend an existing industry or an entrenched way of doing business. *Tech Crunch*, an online publication covering the tech industry, calls its major annual event "Disrupt," as disruption is typically a key ingredient for any startup looking to become the next billion-dollar enterprise.

Think of Zoom disrupting corporate travel and centralized offices. Prior to COVID, it would have been unthinkable to consider a mostly telecommuting workforce. But the necessity to protect ourselves from the virus forced us to find new ways of working. And incredibly, we discovered that not only did Zoom calls allow us to continue to work, but Zoom created productivity gains in eliminating physical commutes.

We also learned that an in-person corporate sales call– which might typically cost thousands of dollars– could be replaced by a virtual call. Who needs to hop on a jet, find a hotel, comp for meals– when an entire sales meeting can be conducted online?

And look at the impact telecommuting has had on commercial real estate. Class A office properties with premier tenants may continue to thrive, but in American city after city, we see Class B spaces struggle to ink new leases.

The capacity to telecommute– with Zoom being the leading app– has likely forever changed commercial real estate, corporate travel, and the way we work together. Now that's disruption.

Amazon– the pioneer of online retail– is also one of the most disruptive companies. Around the country, retail space is shrinking. Malls are closing. Entrenched retailers like Macy's, JCPenney, Bed Bath & Beyond, and Sears are either struggling or shuttered all together.

Many of the most successful companies have been disruptors. Think of the disruption of the old-fashioned taxi service Uber catalyzed. Robinhood forced all the entrenched online stock brokerage firms to drop their commissions to zero. Airbnb has changed how people travel and altered the hospitality industry.

When you are thinking about buying a stock, think about whether it is disrupting an industry. Is the company causing pain for entrenched competitors?

No talk of disruption would be complete without considering Netflix. Younger people think of Netflix strictly as a streaming entertainment service. But for those of us a little bit older, we remember Netflix as the online video rental service that started mailing DVD discs!

Do you recall all of the video rental stores that used to dot every city and town in the country? Video rental giants Blockbuster and Hollywood Video were billion-dollar businesses. At its peak Blockbuster had more than 9,000 stores. Prior to the emergence of Netflix, my little suburb outside Boston with 40,000 people had five video stores and browsing the aisles for a good flick was a commonplace weekend activity.

Netflix, with its revolutionary business model of mail order disc delivery, turned the video rental business on its head. No more strolling aisles to pick the right flick; no more stores. Netflix completely changed the behavior of video rental.

And of course, Netflix didn't stop there. Eventually they realized that high-speed broadband would disrupt sending discs in the mail, so they created a streaming service to upend their own business! And they went one step further– recognizing that streaming itself was simply a commodity, they began creating their own entertainment. This triple disrup-

THE SHARK INVESTOR
DO THIS AND FORGET ABOUT THAT

tion of the entertainment industry is why Netflix has a $200 billion market cap and is one of the great growth stocks of the last 20 years.

CNBC, which we think of being primarily focused on publicly-traded companies, publishes an annual "Disruptors" list of 50 private startups that are looking to "unseat corporate giants."

"CNBC features private companies– from biotech and machine learning to transportation and retail and even exploring outer space– whose innovations are changing the world. These forward-thinking startups have not only identified unexploited niches in the market that have the potential to become billion-dollar businesses, a majority of them already are billion-dollar businesses."

It's good to peruse the list each year to get a look at privately-held companies that may have IPOs and become successful public companies. Make it an exercise– ask yourself– what's special about the business models of the companies that appear on this list?

Do any of the names from the 2018 list sound familiar: Lyft, Uber, SpaceX, Airbnb? Uber and Airbnb are now leading publicly-traded companies. Coinbase and Crowdstrike also were on CNBC's list of 50 Disruptors, and were both big stock market gainers in 2020 and 2021. SpaceX is still private, but sports an eye-popping $210 billion valuation.

If you have any doubts as to whether a disruptive company is a better investment than an incumbent, take a look at the "CNBC Disruptor Index" chart, which tracks firms that appeared on the CNBC list and then later went public. Over the last eight years, the Disruptor Index has trounced the S&P 500 sporting a 370% total return vs. the S&P's (approximate) 170% return. Even compared to the more "techy" and aggressive Nasdaq Composite Index (which tracks 2,500 Nasdaq companies), the Disruptor Index still comes out on top with its 370% return besting the Nasdaq's (approximate) 260%. So, before you invest in an individual stock– ask yourself– "Is this stock pick a disruptive company?"

Buy Companies With Economic Moats

Buy stocks with "economic moats" says Warren Buffett. Just as the moat of a medieval castle repelled invaders, an "economic moat" describes a company's capacity to keep competitors at bay.

Buffett advises investors to find companies with qualities that are difficult for other companies to copy. If something can be easily replicated, then it's hard to protect profit margins.

According to an article published at *GuruFocus.com*, Buffett explained

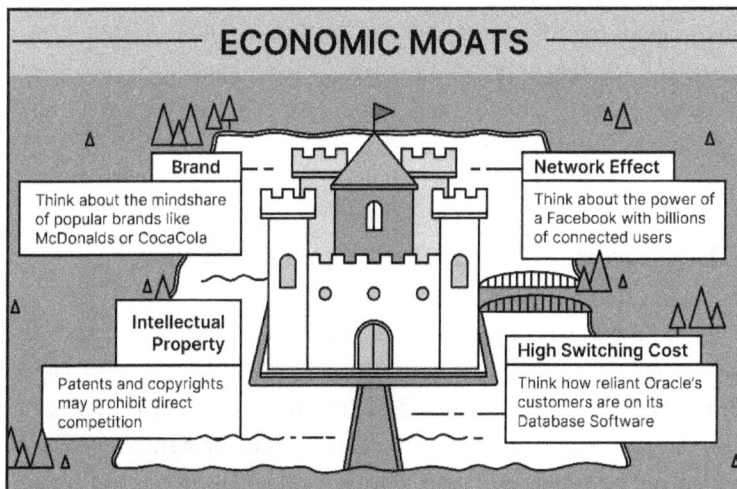

ECONOMIC MOATS

Brand
Think about the mindshare of popular brands like McDonalds or CocaCola

Network Effect
Think about the power of a Facebook with billions of connected users

Intellectual Property
Patents and copyrights may prohibit direct competition

High Switching Cost
Think how reliant Oracle's customers are on its Database Software

his moat principal at the 1995 Berkshire Hathaway (NYSE:BRK.A) annual meeting of shareholders.

"What we're trying to do," he said, answering a question from the audience, "is we're trying to find a business with a wide and long-lasting moat around it…protecting a terrific economic castle with an honest lord in charge of the castle."

What creates an economic moat– these barricades that interdict competitors?

Buffett described some of the qualities that can protect a company: "It can be because it's the low-cost producer in some area, it can be because it has a natural franchise because of surface capabilities, it could be because of its position in the consumers' mind, it can be because of a technological advantage, or any kind of reason at all, that it has this moat around it."

Buffett suggests investors analyze the current reasons the moat exists, and to question if the moat will continue into the future: "Why is that castle still standing? And what's going to keep it standing or cause it not to be standing five, 10, 20 years from now? What are the key factors? And how permanent are they?"

Engage in a Controlled "Spray and Pray"

While somewhat oxymoronic, the controlled "spray and pray" thesis espouses that you don't know which "bullet" will strike its target. Translated to our investments, we don't know which company will grow into the next Apple, Amazon, or Facebook. Thus, we want to "spray" or spread our bets, and then "pray" that we've found the next great company. But we are not "spraying" everywhere. We are controlling and limiting our investments to well-researched companies that possess fast earnings growth, visionary CEOs, and many of the other qualities we've discussed.

And we'll need to be patient. We'll only realize that Jeff Bezos is an amazing genius who can build a $600 billion revenue company *after* he does it. We didn't know this in 1997 when Amazon came public.

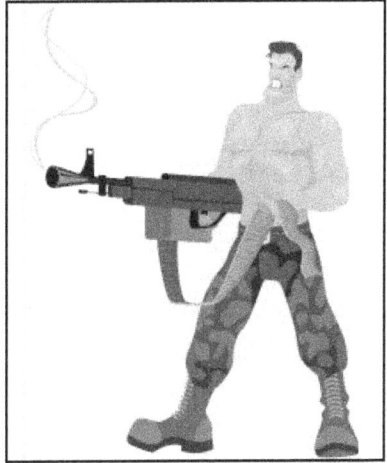

So– have a calculated "spray" of investments in companies where you've done your due diligence. Keep your bets even and have lots of ideas. Try a few different industries.

My suggestion is to patiently build a portfolio of 15-20 picks.

A very concentrated portfolio of individual picks has less likelihood of success. Remember, most stocks underperform the S&P. Just as a Venture Capitalist spreads his or her bets among dozens of startups, you'll probably get better performance by increasing your total number of picks. At the same time, we don't want to engage in over-diversification (as Buffett warns). Stick with industries and companies that you fully understand.

According to a blog post from Craig Lazzara, the Managing Director of Index Investment Strategy at S&P Dow Jones Indices, a bigger portfolio is better than a smaller one: "More diversified portfolios, by including more stocks, stand a better chance of outperformance."

Remember– Venture Capitalists will build portfolios of startups. Out of 10 VC investments, probably three will go to zero; another four to five might return the original investment; and 1-2 produce substantial returns.

That means as a public market investor you've got an advantage over the VCs. Their seed and early stage bets often go to zero with no liquidity. Whereas stocks rarely go to zero, and if they do falter, you can exit via a liquid public market.

Build an Earnings Roadmap

I always find it helpful to develop what I call an "earnings roadmap" in a spreadsheet. It allows an investor the capacity to ascertain a likely scenario of growth for a prospective investment.

With a little knowledge of Excel, one can easily produce a concrete and visual reference point for understanding how a company's earnings will grow and hopefully catalyze a commensurate increasing stock price.

Let's take a look at Facebook (or META) and build an example. If I take a little jaunt through Yahoo! Finance, and click on the "Analysis" tab, I can see that the consensus analysts' estimate for Facebook's earnings growth rate is 23.93% per annum for the next five years. Now I'll scroll up a little in Yahoo! Finance and note that the current year estimate for Facebook's earnings is $18.33.

Perfect, let's combine these two items in Excel. As of this writing Facebook shares are trading for $509.58 with a PE multiple of 34.25.

Facebook (META)	2024	2025	2026	2027	2028
EPS 23.93% growth	$18.33	$22.71	$28.15	$34.88	$43.23
PE of 30	$549.90	$681.30	$844.50	$1,046.40	$1,296.90
PE of 25	$458.25	$567.75	$703.75	$872.00	$1,080.75
	2024	2025	2026	2027	2028
EPS 20.00% growth	$18.33	$21.99	$26.39	$31.67	$38.00
PE of 25	$458.25	$549.75	$659.75	$791.75	$950.00
PE of 20	$366.60	$439.80	$527.80	$633.40	$760.00

So, let's assume Facebook hits the analysts' estimate of $18.33 for 2024, and that the stock has a PE of 30 at some point during the year. Looking at column 2024 (above), we can see that Facebook would trade at $549.90. However, if the stock trades only at a PE of 25, shares would be at $458.25.

Let's continue the progression– if Facebook actually grows earnings at 23.93% per annum for five years, by 2028 the company will sport an EPS figure of $43.23. If we apply a PE multiple of 30 (as seen in the 2028 column), then we could see a stock price of $1,296.90. However, if Facebook only reaches a PE multiple of 25, shares would trade at $1,080.75.

For the second grouping of numbers, I utilized the assumption that Facebook hits the 2024 $18.33 EPS target, but only grows earnings at 20% per annum thereafter. If this more conservative estimate actually materializes, then Facbook will only earn $38.00 per share in 2028. If

I apply a PE multiple of 25, as in the 2028 column, then Facebook will trade at $950.00. A more conservative PE multiple of 20 would yield a $760.00 stock price.

All of these numbers appear reasonably Bullish to me. Based on Facebook's growth rate, as predicted by analysts, the company should grow its earnings at a rapid trajectory. And if the PE multiple is 30 at some point during 2028, an investor should make a 140% return based on the current stock price of $509.58. Even under the most conservative scenario exhibited here– with earnings growth of 20% per annum and a PE of 20– an investor would garner nearly 50% growth.

The most important element of this exercise is that it demonstrates an analytic approach to projecting a company's future stock price as opposed to *wishful*. Any number of things could get in the way of Facebook's business performing well over the five year interval. But if they do hit these projected EPS numbers, an investor should experience an attractive gain.

Forget About Technical Analysis

Incredibly, Wall Street employs professionals known as Technicians or Technical Analysts. These folks claim to be able to divine the future price movement of stocks by looking at the chart of a company's past price movement. They are often very articulate and utilize fascinating terms such as "support levels," "Bollinger Bands," "head and shoulder patterns," "cup and handle" and "resistance levels."

When you listen to a Technical Analyst speak, effortlessly uttering all of these academic-sounding terms, it makes investing in stocks sound like a science!

At surface, we should understand that it is impossible to predict the future of a stock based on its past movement. If it was, then we could all beat the market averages– right? If investing was a science and charts can tell us where a stock is going, the case is closed. We just need to learn the science of the charts, and the future is foretold.

Buffett tried Technical Analysis in his early years until realizing its shortcomings. He reportedly joked about this dilemma with an audience at Vanderbilt University in 2005, "I realized that Technical Analysis didn't work when I turned the chart upside down and didn't get a different answer."

According to a *Forbes* magazine article, two Santa Clara University professors who engaged in a study of traders using Technical Analysis found the investors employing the method had lower performance, on average: approximately 50 basis points (0.5%) *per month* in raw returns from portfolio selection decisions and 20 basis points (0.2%) from additional transaction costs.

The study went on to determine that "individual investors who use technical analysis to make investment decisions are disproportionately prone to speculate on short-term stock-market trends, hold more concentrated portfolios, turn over those securities at a higher rate than

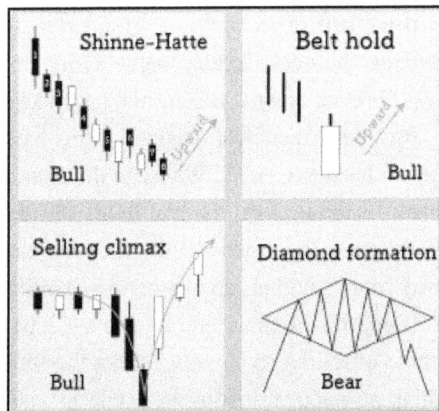

people who do not use charts, and earn lower returns."

Burton Malkiel in his investment classic *A Random Walk Down Wall Street*, explains that Technical Analysis has been thoroughly examined, and proven to be meaningless: "These technical rules have been tested exhaustively by using stock-price data as far back as the beginning of the twentieth century. The results reveal that past movements in stock prices cannot be used reliably to foretell future movements."

Let's be blunt: don't be seduced by this pseudo-science. There is nothing that the past price movement of a stock can do to influence, reveal, determine, or control future movement.

Stocks represent ownership units of a business. The only thing that will make a business become more valuable is if the company's earnings increase.

And the only thing that will make earnings go up is a successfully executed business strategy. Whether that's creating new products, new partnerships, or entering new markets– only increasing profits will make a company more valuable long term.

If we look at a chart of Apple in 2002, every Technician would have avoided the stock like the plague. Using their own terminology, the stock was "broken down." It had sunk past a key "support level."

But these Technical Analysis terms have nothing to do with Apple's actual business, right? Where in the chart does it predict that the company is about to release the iPod, and the iPad, and then its *piece de resistance*– the iPhone? How does the chart tell us that Apple is on its way from a market cap of around $10 billion to $3.0 trillion and beyond?

It doesn't! A chart simply displays past price movement and is incapable of telling us anything about the future of a business. If you were thinking about investing in Apple in 2002, forget about the chart and think about Apple's remarkable CEO: Steve Jobs.

We can sum up our statement on Technical Analysis with Peter Lynch's famously derogatory comment on the field: "Charts are great for predicting the past." Enough said!

Forget About Penny Stocks

An instinct common among beginning investors is to be attracted to "penny" stocks; that is stocks trading below $5.00 per share.

The logic goes something like this: "If I buy 1,000 shares of a $2 per share company, I'll sell when the stock goes to $3.00, and pocket a quick thousand-dollar gain."

If this is how you are prone to think, please go back and re-read the section on understanding market cap.

Remember, the $2.00 or $3.00 share price isn't that meaningful without also knowing how many shares exist. If there are 10 billion shares for a $3.00 stock, the company has a $30 billion dollar market cap. That's a large cap company. So, while the share price is low, it doesn't mean that the company's overall valuation is small.

More important, is that whether the stock is $2.00 or $200.00, it's just as hard for a company's share price to advance from $2.00 to $3.00 as it is to advance from $200.00 to $300.00. It's a 50% move either way. In our example above, it will take a lot of revenue growth to make a $30 billion market cap company turn into a $45 billion one.

In order to advance 50%, a company typically needs to report strong earnings and a positive earnings outlook (meaning the CEO and CFO see bright prospects ahead).

THE SHARK INVESTOR
DO THIS AND FORGET ABOUT THAT

Don't confuse cheapness with value. Yes– in absolute terms a $2.00 share price is cheap in the realm of integers. But it doesn't mean that it's market cap is low, nor does it mean that there's something intrinsically valuable about the company.

When Warren Buffet's Berkshire Hathaway traded at $1,000.00 in 1983 it was actually more likely to double in value than some trashy penny stock trading at $1.00. Why? Because it had a great CEO with great operating companies, a great investment portfolio, and great prospects for earnings growth. And today Berkshire trades north of $600,000!

Also, consider there might be very good reasons why the stock price is low. Where was the stock one year ago, or three years ago? If it's at $2.00 today but was at $20.00 three years ago, it's probably fallen because of poor business prospects. In fact, $1.00 or $2.00 a share might be a quick stop before bankruptcy, and then worthlessness.

So, forget about penny stocks and concentrate on companies that have strong business models, great CEOs, and growing earnings. If you find a company that has strong growth prospects and a $2.00 price tag– great– then more power to you.

But don't let dreams of making a quick buck divert your attention from strong companies to ones with micro share prices.

Be Wary of "Fake" Technology Companies

Ride-hailing upstart Uber is a fascinating, disruptive company, there's no denying it. But I find it interesting that the actual name of the company is "Uber Technologies." I'm going to pick on Uber just a little bit to make a point: investors should learn to discern "fake" technology companies. When I say fake, I mean that the actual business isn't technology. A company may use the word "Technology" in their name, or may add clever suffixes. But that doesn't mean they are a technology company. Technology companies are often awarded handsome P/Es and given long leashes to attain profitability. It's no wonder then that other non-technology, money losing ventures like to co-opt the term and masquerade as technology companies.

In the late 1990s a rash of companies added ".com" to their name to sell themselves as internet concerns. Today, firms are adding AI to their brands to garner attention and capitalize on the interest in Artificial Intelligence. When you think you might be buying a technology company, ask yourself what is the underlying product or service? Is the company producing software or semiconductors, or something distinctly more mundane.

Let's take a look at Uber "Technologies." Yes– you utilize an app to connect a person seeking a ride to a driver and a car, but the actual service is a taxi company. Prior to mobile phones, we got on the phone and requested a car. Or in urban areas, we raised our hand or whistled and hailed a cab. And taxi services were never considered high margin businesses. And speaking of margin (as in Profit Margin), it took Uber 14 years and $32 billion of cumulative losses before reaching its first profitable quarter in 2023! The Venture Capitalists who were early backers of Uber made out, but the early investors in Uber's IPO have waited five years on a stock that has underperformed the S&P in the same time period.

Let's give Uber credit– any company that becomes a verb (as in – "I think I'll Uber it to your place") deserves props. They disrupted an old school industry and created a near global brand for finding a ride. *But it's*

THE SHARK INVESTOR
DO THIS AND FORGET ABOUT THAT

just a taxi and delivery service. And research group IBISWorld estimates that the U.S. taxi and limousine industry generates an average profit margin of 2.7%. This 2.7% is a far cry from the profit margins generated from software, semiconductors, and other tech segments.

Teladoc was a high-flying name in 2021 that deserves further examination. According to their website, they describe themselves as thus: "Teladoc Health is the global leader in whole-person virtual care—offering the technology to connect, expertise you can trust and the power to improve health for all." When I look through Teladoc's web site, it becomes difficult for me to discern exactly what they provide? Do they employ doctors? Do they have laboratories? When my foot hurt from a soccer fall, I needed to get a *real* X-Ray, not a virtual one. In order to get over a rotator cuff injury, I needed to see a real physical therapist with actual exercise equipment. Surprisingly, I've had some tele-health consults with physicians and none of them used Teladoc to power their patient communications. In my mind the real assets in healthcare are the physicians, nurses, labs, and diagnostic and surgical equipment that allow patients to be treated. A *conduit* to a health provider seems like a far less valuable service. In 2022 the company reported $2.4 billion in revenue (which sounds pretty good), but losses ran a staggering $13.6 billion.

Perhaps the most infamous "fake" technology company is WeWork, the office co-working outfit forced to scrap an IPO due to a lack of investor interest. WeWork co-founder, Adam Neumann, must be an incredibly charismatic and persuasive individual. From WeWork's founding in 2010 until 2019, Neumann was able to convince investors that WeWork was something more than a Real Estate shop. Attracting financing faster than Brad Pitt attracts admirers, WeWork landed top-tier investors such as J.P. Morgan Chase, T. Rowe Price, Wellington Management, Goldman Sachs, and Harvard.

WeWork's business model was simple: the startup signed long-term leases in class A office buildings in major cities and allowed startups and other interested companies to lease space on a flexible, short-term basis. WeWork offered common amenities like exercise rooms and free beer.

Neumann's greatest sales job– potentially the greatest sales job in this millennium– came in when he convinced Softbank CEO Masayoshi Son to invest $10 billion (over time) in WeWork, cresting at a $47 billion valuation. WeWork was annualizing about $3.5 billion in revenue but sporting losses of nearly $4 billion! Why would anyone pay $47 billion for a company that was losing more money than it was taking in? In its IPO filing WeWork disclosed it was on the hook for $47 billion of future lease obligations, but had only $4 billion of future lease commitments. In other words– insolvent.

Part of the seduction process was Neumann's insistence that WeWork was a technology company. In a 2019 article titled "No, WeWork Isn't a Tech Company. Here's Why That Matters," *Harvard Business Review* noted WeWork used the word "technology" 110 times in its IPO prospectus. Thankfully, the potential IPO buy side customers– mutual funds and hedge funds– sniffed out that they were getting duped, and put the breaks on assisting WeWork in selling itself to the public.

The *Harvard Business Review* article noted several characteristics that real technology companies have, most important of which is scale. Technology companies have significant intellectual property, and once a product or service is created, it can be utilized with little increase in cost. Facebook creates a centralized piece of software that billions of people utilize. The same for Google.

WeWork, Uber, and online retailers like Chewy (pet products) and

THE SHARK INVESTOR
DO THIS AND FORGET ABOUT THAT

Instacart (grocery delivery) lack scalability. For every tenant WeWork signs, they need to provide costly space (and free beer). For every passenger hailing a ride, Uber needs to send a driver and a car. For every grocery order Instacart receives, they need to get the groceries, get a car, get a driver, and deliver it to the customer's home. These are pretty much zero-scale business models.

There is a certain amount of hucksterism in publicly traded markets. We saw this in the Dot Com period when companies were rapidly thrown together, employees hired at breakneck speed, and IPOs were branding events. Losing money was an advantage. A Dot Com could claim that unimaginable profits were down the road. If a company actually had profits, investors might question what the appropriate P/E should be.

As an investor– beware! No one is really on your side. You must be highly discerning about companies and their business models. Adam Neumann had no qualms about telling anyone who would listen that WeWork was a unique "technology" company. Now bankrupt, we can clearly see that WeWork was a pig with lipstick. In Neumann's case we learned the emperor had no clothes, but not before he managed to wrangle a personal payout of $1.7 billion dollars from Softbank.

Forget About "Meme" Stocks

In the first two years after the pandemic, every time I ran an investment class where we played a stock market game, someone would inevitably buy GameStop and/or AMC Entertainment for their portfolio.

No matter how much negative information is published about these companies, and no matter how much I suggest that the class focus on companies with growing earnings, my student investors just appear to be attracted to these Meme stocks.

I believe the catalyst for this behavior is the same instinct that drives FOMO (fear of missing out). Because there is such noise around the Meme names, and because they've read that someone made a lot of money quickly, inexperienced investors can't resist dipping their toes in the water, hoping that they can get rich quick as well.

This instinct is well entrenched in many investors. They would rather think of the stock market as a casino– a place where they can get lucky and make a big fortune.

A deeper analysis of the Meme stock craze reveals how dangerous it is for most investors.

The peculiar trend of Meme stock investing arose in the COVID-induced stock market mania of late 2020 and 2021. The behavior of mostly inexperienced players catapulted a handful of firms with limited growth

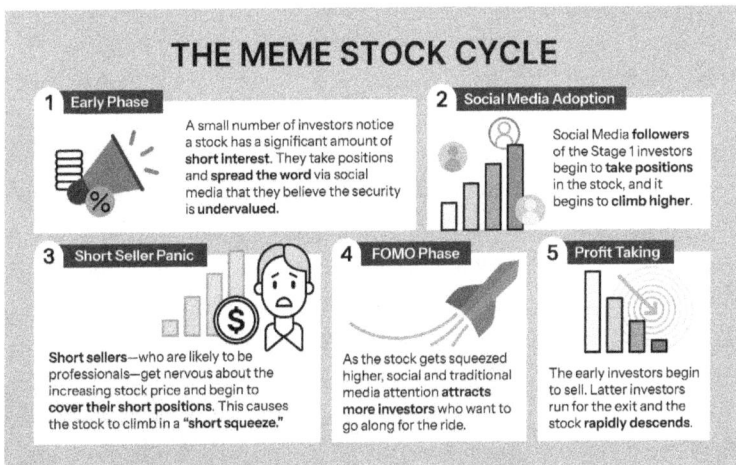

THE MEME STOCK CYCLE

1 Early Phase
A small number of investors notice a stock has a significant amount of **short interest**. They take positions and **spread the word** via social media that they believe the security is **undervalued**.

2 Social Media Adoption
Social Media **followers** of the Stage 1 investors begin to **take positions** in the stock, and it begins to **climb higher**.

3 Short Seller Panic
Short sellers—who are likely to be professionals—get nervous about the increasing stock price and begin to **cover their short positions**. This causes the stock to climb in a **"short squeeze."**

4 FOMO Phase
As the stock gets squeezed higher, social and traditional media attention **attracts more investors** who want to go along for the ride.

5 Profit Taking
The early investors begin to sell. Latter investors run for the exit and the stock **rapidly descends**.

prospects to national headlines, made money for a small number of investors, and ushered in a new wave of herd investing.

The premise for Meme investing works as follows: target a company with a large short interest (which means that many investors believe the stock is going down). Start buying the stock and spread your bullish opinion to other investors utilizing social media. If herd buying pushes the stock upwards, the shorts must cover their positions, which in turn pushes the stock higher. This ultimately results in a "short squeeze" where the investors with short positions clamor to quickly buy back shares and the price is pushed upward in a hockey stick fashion. This operation was illustrated in the film "Dumb Money."

GameStop was arguably ground zero for Meme investing. An important point to understand about the GameStop saga is that the main individual investor fingered to have actually made a substantial amount of money in GameStop stock was a professional, Keith Gill. Mr. Gill is a highly educated investor possessing the CFA (Chartered Financial Analyst) designation, which typically requires years of study. The other big winners in the GameStop craze were institutions: mutual fund companies like Fidelity and BlackRock, and hedge funds (like the one owned by Ryan Cohen).

This process of identifying stocks with substantial short interest, and then crowding in to push the stock higher, was repeated with other companies such as AMC, Nokia, Blackberry, and Bed Bath & Beyond.

Mr. Gill bought his initial shares in 2019, with an average acquisition price around $5.00, more than a year before the GameStop craze began. He certainly benefited from the eventual mass herd trampling into the stock, and at one point his brokerage statements (revealed to reporters) exhibited a position worth tens of millions of dollars. But what happened to the average investor who bought a Meme stock?

Popular investment website *Motley Fool* surveyed 1,500 investors in the United States around the time of the GameStop craze. Incredibly, more than half of the investors surveyed had purchased a Meme stock recommended on the Reddit subgroup r/wallstreetbets.

According to the survey, 30% of the respondents don't actually understand short selling that much.

And where is GameStop today? As of this writing, shares are trading at around $22.00, down substantially from its peak trading price of $120.00. Can you imagine how many investors bought at prices well north of the current $22.00. AMC Entertainment (NYSE:AMC) was another Meme craze darling with a big short interest that lured investors at prices between $30.00 and $565. AMC shares now hover around $5.00. Suffice to say, there are likely thousands of investors who got the short end of the stick.

Forget About Margin (Borrowing Money)

Investors are often tempted to add some gasoline to their investments by purchasing securities on margin, or using borrowed money (from the brokerage firm). This is generally a bad idea for the individual investor. Gasoline itself is double-edged: it can add power, but it can also go up in flames. Buying on margin– while capable of supercharging your investment returns– can lead to implosion.

The general principle is that you can control a larger number of shares by borrowing money. Let's say an investor has $5,000 in their account, and they are attracted to XYZ Security trading at $100.00 per share.

THE SHARK INVESTOR
DO THIS AND FORGET ABOUT THAT

They are allowed to borrow up to 50% of the purchase value, so they can buy $10,000 worth of stock. $5,000 comes from their cash in the account, and the other $5,000 is borrowed from the brokerage firm.

If the stock doubles in value, the investor now has a $20,000 position. If they sell at the $20,000 mark, they pay off the $5,000 they borrowed (plus interest that accrued) and are now sitting on $15,000 in equity– a tripling of their initial $5,000 investment.

This is the rosiest of all possible scenarios.

What happens if the stock goes down? Let's say an investor buys 100 shares of a high-flying Meme stock at $100.00 a share. They invest $5,000 and borrow another $5,000. Unfortunately, the investor was late to the party and the Meme stock that just had a rocket ship ride up now plummets, and is at $20.00 a share. The investor now has a $2,000 equity position, and a $5,000 debt to the brokerage firm (on which he or she is paying interest). The brokerage firm will want their money, and the investor will receive a "maintenance" call to increase the equity in the account to a certain level.

It should be plainly obvious that buying on margin is a highly combustible business. Investing in individual stocks is risky enough. You never know what a stock is going to do in the next 30 to 180 days. Stocks can lose 50% of their value at any moment. War can break out, there can be a terrorist attack, the Fed can raise rates, a company can report horrific earnings. If you buy 100 shares of a $100.00 stock with $10,000.00 of cash and it goes to $20.00, you've still got $2,000.00 of equity. And you can sit on that position as long as you want. However, if you buy stock with the brokerage firm's money, and the stock plummets, not only does your equity get wiped out, but you're indebted to the brokerage firm that made the loan.

Mercifully, through something known as Regulation T, the Federal Reserve Board currently limits the amount of a security that can be borrowed by an investor to 50% of the initial position. Fifty percent may seem like a decent safety cushion, but as the above example illustrates, a strong unexpected downward move may leave a margin investor underwater.

Warren Buffett warned of the dangers of using margin. "There is simply no telling how far stocks can fall in a short period," he wrote in his 2017 annual letter to shareholders. "Even if your borrowings are small and your positions aren't immediately threatened by the plunging market, your mind may well become rattled by scary headlines and breathless commentary."

A personal friend of mine who bought on margin during the Dot Com boom ended up with a sad story. He had originally invested $75K across a handful of high-flying internet names, and juiced up his portfolio by borrowing another 75K. At the internet bubble's peak his portfolio was worth 300K, and he was celebrating with steak dinners followed by cigars and single malt scotches. However, when the market swooned and his stocks lost 90% of their value, he was left with only 30K in stocks, and margin debt of 75K. Needless to say, he was not a happy camper (and neither was his wife).

Forget About Market Gurus

Should you listen to market gurus– you know, the talking heads dispensing advice that appear regularly on CNBC or Fox Business News? They seem smart and articulate, and make pronouncements about individual stocks or market direction with categorical certainty.

They issue absolute declarations like: BUY this and SELL that, or the Dow is going to 50,000 by year end!

They make these assertions with such confidence they must be right, right? Or, right most of the time?

Well, research performed by the CXO Advisory Group and cited by the publication *Wealth Management*, suggests that the market gurus probably aren't worth following.

"The CXO Advisory Group set out to determine if stock market 'experts,' whether self-proclaimed or endorsed by others, reliably provide useful stock market timing guidance. To find the answer, from 2005 through 2012, they collected and investigated 6,584 forecasts for the U.S. stock market offered publicly by 68 experts: Bulls and Bears employing technical, fundamental and sentiment indicators. They selected experts, based on web searches of public archives, with enough forecasts spanning enough market conditions to gauge accuracy."

The study concluded: "Across all forecasts, accuracy was worse than the flip of a coin– on average, just under 47%."

You'll experience the same odds playing at a Blackjack table. You'll win some, but if you keep betting, you're going to lose all of your money.

Well known guru Jim Cramer, the brilliant and entertaining CNBC personality and prognosticator, came in at 47%.

Abby Joseph Cohen, the long-time chief investment strategist at Goldman Sachs, finished her career at a rather unimpressive 35%.

Lesson learned– no one can predict the price movement of a stock or market direction with significant accuracy.

Forget About Options...Mostly

If you think you are going to get rich quickly trading options, you should give it a second thought. There are innumerable books, videos, and live courses that claim to teach winning options strategies. Please pause and consider that if it was easy to get rich trading options, wouldn't we all be using these strategies? I think the average investor can apply the same doubt to options as they might apply to Technical Analysis– if these strategies really work, wouldn't we all just follow them?

Options– a form of a derivative– can make or lose money for investors based on the movement of an underlying security. There is a large assortment of books published on understanding options, so we won't get into all the details here. But very simply: Buying a Call option allows an investor to profit if a stock goes up; and Buying a Put option allows an investor to profit if a stock goes down. A buyer of an option contract (which consists of 100 shares) pays a fee to own the contract– and this fee is known as the Premium. On the other side of the trade is the Writer of the contract, who receives the premium from the Buyer.

Options can be very good tools for people who either want to 1) Protect against downside risk by Buying Puts; or 2) Generate returns by Writing Calls.

Both of these strategies can be employed with little risk when an investor actually *owns the underlying stock*. As an example, if I own 100 shares of XYZ and I'm sitting on a 100% gain in the stock, I could buy a Put. And if the price of XYZ goes down, I've hedged my bet with the profits I'll make from the Put. Conversely, if I own XYZ, I could Write a Call option, and collect the Premium from the investor who bought the Call. If the stock goes down or does nothing, the contract expires worthless to the Call Buyer. But the Call Writer pockets the Premium. If the stock goes up such that the option contract is exercised, then the Call Writer sells the shares to the Call Buyer at the contract price.

Yes– this is confusing. If you've never studied options before, you'll need to find a guide that walks you through it step by step. But I would avoid options investing unless you're Buying Puts to protect a position, or Writing Calls to generate income.

There are an infinite number of options strategies with fascinating names such as "Bull Call Spread," "Protective Collar," and a "Long Strangle." But all of them are far riskier than actually owning shares of stock in a company.

Let's do some very simple math. What are the odds that a stock goes up or down? 50% likelihood of going up, and a 50% likelihood of going down. But with a typical option, you are betting that a security will go up or down within a certain time period. By adding a time delineator, you've added an additional obstacle to your bet. Not only do you have to be correct that the security goes up, but it has to go up a minimum amount, within a certain period of time.

If I buy $10,000 worth of XYZ security, the stock might do nothing for six months. But if I'm patient, maybe the company gets acquired at a 35% premium seven months after my initial purchase price. And I'm rewarded for my patience. But if I buy a Call option betting that XYZ shares increase within six months, and they instead stay flat, my option is essentially worthless to me.

And remember that with a Call option, you need for the stock to not only just go up, it has to go up a certain amount. This is analogous to a 6.5 point spread in a sports bet– you're not just betting that the Dallas Cowboys win, but they have to win by a touchdown!

A study jointly conducted by MIT and Stanford professors revealed that retail options traders tend to make important wealth *depleting* mistakes translating to losses in a range of 5% to 9% for trading options around earnings announcements, and even more (10% to 14%) for those with high expected volatility.

A University of Florida study found that "less sophisticated and overly confident retail investors tend to lose money on trading complex options with shrouded risks."

John Train in his classic *The New Money Masters* paraphrases Peter Lynch's take on options: "The options market is a gigantic, useless, gambling casino." Once again– don't be seduced by options trading and the idea of getting rich quick. If it were easy, we'd all be doing it.

Forget About Active Investing or Day Trading

One of the many "get rich quick" strategies employed by investors is Active Investing or Day Trading. The underlying thesis of this strategy is that an investor makes a lot of trades, getting in and out positions quickly; and closes out his/her trades by the end of the day (as not to be surprised by overnight news that may affect the positions). An investor might open the day buying Apple, and sell it minutes

THE SHARK INVESTOR
DO THIS AND FORGET ABOUT THAT

later if it shows an increase in price.

These investors are often company agnostic. In fact, they often avoid learning about companies (e.g. utilizing Fundamental Analysis), and instead supplant the due diligence process with charts, believing they can glean insight into future price movement by studying past movement and volume levels.

Unfortunately, many of the major brokerage firms run ads glorifying Day Trading as a legitimate and glamorous way to make money. Some commercials even suggest an investor quit his/her job, become their "own boss," and generate daily income with their successful active trades. They show a good looking guy with his arms folded behind his back smiling at his three trading screens with red and green lights blinking away. If only it were so easy!

Statistics cited at TradeSociety.com, which is a resource for Day Traders, paint a horrible picture of the likelihood of success for persons who pursue active trading:

1. 80% of all day traders quit within the first two years.
2. Among all day traders, nearly 40% day trade for only one month. Within three years, only 13% continue to day trade. After five years, only 7% remain.
3. Traders sell winners at a 50% higher rate than losers. 60% of sales are winners, while 40% of sales are losers.
4. The average individual investor underperforms a market index by 1.5% per year. Active traders underperform by 6.5% annually.
5. Day Traders with strong past performance go on to earn strong returns in the future. Though only about 1% of all Day Traders are able to predictably profit net of fees.

I personally know that active investing is a great way to not only lose your money, but your marriage as well. One friend left a cushy gig as an IT professional at a Downtown Boston law firm. He was making six figures while staring out over the Boston seaport. He left these comfortable digs to actively Day Trade (from his basement) the money he had saved up. Of course, he used margin, and quickly lost all of his equity, and created tens of thousands of dollars of debt for himself.

Another friend was Day Trading high flying technology stocks during the Dot Com boom. He kept telling everyone that he was doing well, but it turned out he was losing most of the family's liquid savings. He not only lost the savings, but lost the wife as well.

Remember, don't focus on trying to make quick money! Active trading will more than likely lead to significant market underperformance, and its impact on your life overall may be even worse!

Think Twice About Consumer Subscription Stocks

A business model I'd be wary of is the consumer subscription. Firms that would fall under this category are Ancestry, Weight Watchers, Blue Apron, StitchFix, etc.

Number one– these firms typically have very high customer acquisition costs; that is they must constantly advertise for new customers. Why? Because the lifespan of a subscription customer is often quite short.

For how long does someone stay on a diet? For how long does someone search for their ancestors? For how long does someone get a box of fancy clothes sent to them each month? These services are often the first expenses a consumer sheds when there is a recession.

The business model is the complete opposite of a bank, where once you deposit your money, you are highly reluctant to change financial institutions.

An exception to this rule is a firm like Netflix, which offers a low-priced service and delivers unique entertainment that cannot be found elsewhere.

This is much different than dieting– people hate dieting! They might enjoy it for 30 days or even 90 days, but they will most likely get off the diet and cancel their Weight Watcher's (Nasdaq:WW) subscription.

So, the key here is analyzing consumer behavior, the pricing, and the subscription durability. Disney Plus and Netflix offer content people love to consume. It cannot be duplicated elsewhere and the pricing is very reasonable.

StitchFix (Nasdaq: SFIX), on the other hand, offers clothing brands like Columbia and Calvin Klein that can be bought at an infinite number of retailers. The pricing would be considered moderate to upper moderate. It might be fun for awhile to get a box shipped to you with a surprise, but there is simply nothing compelling about the offering.

It bears repeating many of these subscriptions are often the first things canceled during a recession, or for whatever reason a consumer finds himself/herself financially squeezed: job loss, missed bonus, career anxiety, divorce, etc.

Forget About Short Selling

Short selling is an investment strategy whereby an investor profits if a stock goes down. And by the way, going *long* a security is what most investors do: they buy stock hoping it goes up.

Thankfully, research indicates that the vast majority of short selling is conducted by institutions and individual investors account for only 2% of the activity. I don't want to spend a lot of time on the whole process of short selling– as I believe it's an endeavor to avoid– but here are the basics:

An investor borrows shares from his broker and they are sold. Let's say that the investor was keen on a $50.00 stock called XYZ he/she thinks is overvalued (and ripe to decline). The investor's account is credited with $5,000 (from the borrowed shares that were sold). Now the investor owes the brokerage firm 100 shares of XYZ stock. They

HOW SHORT SELLING WORKS

1. An investor believes a stock is going down in value and borrows shares from their brokerage firm.

2. The investor sells the borrowed shares and the cash is deposited in their account. The broker charges interest on the borrowed shares.

3. If the stock falls, the investor buys the shares back and returns them to the broker. The investor pockets the difference between the prices.

4. However, if the stock increases in value, the brokerage firm will demand repayment. The investor must buy the shares back and loses money.

will also pay an interest fee on the 100 shares ($5,000) they borrowed.

The investor believes XYZ stock will drop to $25.00. If it does, the investor will purchase 100 shares of XYZ at $25.00 and return the stock to the broker. The investor pays off the debt, and his/her account will have a profit of $2,500. If you're confused by all this activity, don't worry– so was I the first time I was exposed to the concept.

What's important to remember is that the absolute maximum amount of money you can make shorting a stock is 100%. And for that to happen, the stock would have to go all the way to zero, which rarely happens.

What's so great about making 100% if your strategy goes perfectly well, versus potentially making 200,000% owning Monster Beverage?

Additionally, short sellers are at risk if the stock goes up!

As Pavel Savor and Mario Gamboa-Cavazos (researchers from DePaul and Harvard) noted in a paper published in 2011, the risk is asymmetric for short investing versus long investing: "Short sellers may be especially exposed to the risk of their positions moving against them. An investor with a long position can simply choose to wait out a price decline."

For short sellers, if the stock goes up, they have to return those shares at the higher price. Let's consider XYZ. If after six months the stock has moved from $50.00 to $100.00, now the short seller owes the brokerage firm an additional $5,000 (as the shares are now twice as expensive). If the brokerage firm is concerned about the mounting debt, they may force a closing of the position, and the short seller must immediately buy the shares.

Conversely, an investor who is long a security that goes down has no such pressure. He or she can always wait out the downturn.

Be Willing to Buy Unprofitable Companies

Investors willing to dip their toes into the risky waters of unprofitable companies may end up with bigger rewards. One caveat– performing due diligence on an unprofitable company is much more difficult. With no E (as in earnings), you can't figure out a P/E nor a PEG. There is no Profit Margin to scrutinize. And essentially all of your other metrics that analyze *return* fall by the wayside. Return means profitability, so there is no return on assets, or return on equity.

When a company is not profitable, it's possible that its valuation will be depressed relative to profitable peers. After all, some mutual funds and institutions will simply not invest in unprofitable companies.

Additionally, companies must post a profit to be added to the S&P 500. And once a company does post profits, and is potentially added to a major index, the stock price may increase significantly.

Case in point: think of when Tesla was added to the S&P. The announcement was made early November of 2020. Before the announcement, shares in the EV automaker traded at around $135.00 per share. After the announcement of admittance to the S&P, shares immediately rocketed to around $300.00 per share.

If you've never looked at an income statement of a publicly traded company, it's a good idea to try and get a handle on some of the basic principles of Financial Accounting. Buffett stated that "accounting is the language of business." There are several good books on the subject (such as *Financial Accounting for Dummies*), and Peter Lynch has a nice primer in *One Up On Wall Street* in the chapter "Some Famous Numbers."

Being able to understand a few important numbers in a financial statement is akin to having at least modest familiarity with what's under the hood of your car. Such as, could you identify the windshield wiper fluid container? Or, could you check the oil or add water to the radiator? Developing a basic understanding of the financial statements of a company in which you're considering investing thousands of dollars provides the same obvious benefits of possessing basic knowledge of what's under the car hood (in case you need to add windshield fluid or check the oil).

When I'm looking at unprofitable companies, I think it's very important to investigate the reason(s) the company is losing money. Is it because of too much debt, a bloated workforce, high cost of goods sold, etc.? The very first line you'll see on the income statement is the Revenue or Sales figure– also known as the "Top Line." The second line is also very important, and generally reads "Cost of Revenue" or "Cost of Goods Sold."

Let's apply this idea to a furniture retailer, where we'd likely see the term Cost of Goods Sold on the income statement. The furniture store buys its furniture from furniture manufacturers and puts the pieces in a showroom. The money the retailer spends to buy the furniture from manufacturers is the retailer's Cost of Goods Sold, or Cost of Sales, or Cost of Revenue. These terms all mean the same thing.

Palantir	12/31/2023	12/31/2022	12/31/2021
Total Revenue	$2,225,012	$1,905,871	$1,541,889
Cost of Revenue	$431,105	$408,549	$339,404
Gross Profit	$1,793,907	$1,497,322	$1,202,485

Source: Yahoo! Finance

This is perhaps more abstract when thinking about a software company, but lets take a look at the Income Statement of Palantir (Nasdaq:PLTR)

– a company that combs data for governments and corporations. For the year ending 2023, you'll see (in the chart above) that the very first line is the Total Revenue (quoted in thousands), which was $2.225 billion. The next line is Cost of Revenue, which basically tells you, how much money the company spent to build and distribute its product.

What is really important about these two numbers is not the absolute values, but the relative value between them. The question is, what percentage of total revenue (the Top Line) does the Cost of Revenue constitute? This percentage is known as the gross margin. If a furniture retailer does $10 million in sales and the furniture costs them $6 million, then the gross margin is 40%.

For Palantir, we can see that the cost of revenue was $431 million. Let's subtract the $431 million from the $2.225 billion in total revenue, and we get $1.794 billion, that's the third line listed: Gross Profit. And then let's divide $1.794 billion (gross profit) by $2.225 billion (total revenue) and we'll get the gross profit *margin* of a little over 80%.

The 80% gross profit margin is actually a very strong number. It means that it doesn't cost Palantir a lot of money to produce its product. In fact, an 80% gross margin is more than double the overall average of 36.2% for all industries, and even 26 percentage points higher than the software industry in general. As a potential investor in Palantir, this 80% gross margin figure gives me confidence in the likelihood of future success. Compare Palantir's 80% gross profit with a company like automaker Rivian, which reported a -39% gross margin for Q2 of 2024. A negative gross margin means that Rivian is losing money (about $30K) on every vehicle it sells.

While Palantir certainly didn't suffer from a lack of recognition from Wall Street, there are many money managers who will not consider adding an unprofitable company to their portfolio. And the less attention from Wall Street often coincides with a better potential valuation when making your investment. As Peter Lynch advised, buy companies that the analysts and fund managers *don't* follow. Palantir, which was founded in 2003, lost money for 20 years. In February of 2024, Palantir posted its first annual profit (due to strong demand for its AI solutions), which sent shares soaring 31%. When it was announced (September of 2024) that Palantir would be added to the S&P 500, shares popped more than 20%.

When there is no E (earnings), then there is no P/E or PEG to look at. This will scare off a lot of investors. But if you're willing to do some additional research, buying a company before it turns profitable (think Amazon, Tesla, and Spotify) might be a strong move.

Use Market Orders When Buying Stocks, And Here's Why...

You've performed your Fundamental Analysis and Top Down Analysis, and you've considered all of the stock picking elements discussed in this book– and you're certain that you're ready to make an investment. You've logged onto your online broker and you've entered the stock symbol and number of shares that you want to buy. After all that– you'll be presented with another variable. You'll need to click on whether you want to place a Limit Order or a Market Order. A Market Order means you'll receive the best possible price at the moment you enter your order. It typically ensures execution, but not at a specific price.

A Limit Order means that you put in a dollar figure *below* what the stock is currently trading at. And if the stock actually does trade down to the figure you've stipulated, then your order will be transacted at the price you've specified or *better*. It cannot be higher.

So, imagine that a stock is trading at $35.00. You've determined that its PE of 20 is very reasonable considering the company is expected to grow its earnings at 25% for the next 5 years (imputing a PEG of .8). And you say to yourself: "Hey, $35.00 is pretty good, but why not put in a Limit Order of $33.00? I'll show the market what a shrewd bargain hunter I am, and I'll get this sucker at a cheaper price."

If you do so, you will not buy the stock immediately. Instead, you'll delay your purchase until the share price reaches $33.00 or lower. *If it ever* reaches that price point.

I strongly advise against taking such an action.

First off, consider that we are not Day Traders. If you're following the "Shark Investor" thesis, you're looking for a long-term winner. It won't really matter if you pick up a stock at $33.00 vs. $35.00 if you're thinking about quadrupling your money! And that's what you should be contemplating. If you buy a company with strong earnings growth, with a great CEO, in a fantastic market, all at a good price– then you should think about not just doubling your investment but likely quadrupling it over 3-7 years.

Saving a couple of dollars on the initial purchase price simply won't have a significant impact.

Still, you're thinking– "I get it– I'm going to hold for a long time, but why not at least try to get a little bit better value?"

Here's a little story to convince you to just place the Market Order.

It was Thanksgiving Day in 1997. I have a large family in the Boston area with whom I typically celebrate the holiday. In this group I have

THE SHARK INVESTOR
DO THIS AND FORGET ABOUT THAT

four first cousins, three of whom are brothers.

Shortly after greeting me for the holiday, Cousin #1 (as we'll refer to him) said "Michael, what's your pick for this year? I've done so well with Cisco, which you suggested last year."

It just so happened that Cousin #1 was asking for my advice at a very opportune time. I was planning on launching my business publication *Massachusetts Investor's Digest* in March of 1998. I was doing a substantial amount of research on Massachusetts publicly-traded companies, and was preparing to write a feature called "Scintillating Stocks."

One of the companies that would make this launch feature was a little-known company (at that time) called CMGI. Everyone was familiar with a company called Lycos, one of the leading search engines. But very few were cognizant of the fact that CMGI had funded the development of Lycos and held a controlling interest. In fact, CMGI was a mini-conglomerate of Internet companies; a digital Berkshire Hathaway (if you will). Besides its stake in Lycos, it also held large positions in GeoCities, PlanetAll, Reel.com, and dozens of other companies.

In late November, CMGI was trading around $22.00 a share. Cousin #1 didn't need a lot of convincing to buy the stock. The story sounded compelling, and he felt confident having already made plenty of money in other picks I had given him over the years. He went ahead and took a position the next day, buying approximately 300 shares.

As I mentioned, Cousin #1 has two brothers, and they love competing with each other. One of the brothers, whom we'll call Cousin #2, learned about the CMGI recommendation, and was also interested in picking up shares. He had recently made a $2,000 contribution to his IRA. He didn't want to buy an "odd lot" (less than 100 shares) of CMGI, so he put in a Limit Order of 100 shares to buy CMGI at $20.00. The trade would

execute only if CMGI dropped down to $20.00.

It just so happened that shortly after Cousin #1 made his investment, and Cousin #2 placed his Limit Order, that CMGI announced both Microsoft and Intel were each taking 4.9% stakes in the company.

With the news that tech Goliaths Microsoft and Intel were taking positions in CMGI, the shares immediately popped. Cousin #1 who had simply bought the shares was feeling excited. Cousin #2, who waited around for his $20.00 Limit Order price, never saw the trade get executed. CMGI never got down to $20.00 for the Limit Order to be activated.

Let's shape the drama: Cousin #1 has made a $6,600 investment in CMGI, and Cousin #2 is sitting on the sidelines due to his unfulfilled Limit Order.

So what happened? Upon the news that CMGI had retained investors like Microsoft and Intel, the stock popped 18% to $28.50. So, besides never executing at $20.00, the stock became increasingly more expensive for Cousin #2.

But that's just the start of the drama. The late fall of 1997 became one of the important legs of the Internet boom. CMGI and its majority owned Lycos saw their shares rise rapidly. Continuing to climb in value into 1998, and ballooning even more in 1999 and 2000, CMGI became one of the poster stocks for the Dot Com bubble. Lycos grew into one of the Internet's top four most visited web properties, and eventually was acquired for $12.5 billion.

Other CMGI portfolio companies prospered as well. The aforementioned GeoCities was scooped up by Yahoo! for $3.57 billion, PlanetAll was acquired by Amazon, and Reel.com was purchased by Hollywood Video.

The success of these portfolio companies, as well as many others, catapulted CMGI stock into the stratosphere. At one point Cousin #1 was up 100x on his investment!

And Cousin #2– he just sat on the sidelines, kicking himself for never having bought CMGI shares at its Market price. Cousin #1 retained all the bragging rights for stock picking, while Cousin #2 languished in humiliation, having missed the opportunity to make a small fortune in CMGI.

Lesson learned: exert your shrewdness with your initial research and due diligence. When you've found a stock you like at a decent price: BUY IT. You're not at a Moroccan bazaar. So don't be like Cousin #2 and waste your time "haggling" for a better price with a wishful Limit Order.

PART VII

YOU'RE THE ANALYST

BEFORE YOU BUY A HOUSE, you hire an inspector to inspect the house: to look at the roof, the furnace, the basement, the attic, etc. They check for termites, foundation cracks, and other issues. Before you buy a used car, you'll likely take it to a mechanic and they will inspect multiple aspects of the car. Who's performing the inspection of your stock picks? You are! You're the analyst.

Please utilize this three-part "Stock Inspection" checklist (summarizing the concepts we've discussed) consisting of Fundamental Analysis, Top Down Analysis, and Business Quality Analysis before you actually purchase shares of a company.

FUNDAMENTAL ANALYSIS CHECKLIST

Filter #1: Do you understand the company? Do you buy the product or service? Do you love it? Do you see others buying the product? Can you articulate the differences between your prospective pick and its competitors?

Filter #2: Are the earnings growing quickly? If it's less than 15%, why bother? Remember you'll likely earn 10% per annum in the S&P 500 and

15% in a fund like QQQ (see page 191).

Filter #3: What is the PE? If the P/E is above 20, you'll need to look for a commensurate earnings growth rate (move to PEG).

Filter #4: What is the PEG? If it's above 2, it's getting pricey. If it's 4 or above, you may be heading toward nosebleed territory. If it's 1.25 or below, you've probably found a decent value.

Filter #5: Who is the CEO? Are they the Founder? How much stock do they own? How much do they pay themselves?

Filter #6: What is the Profit Margin? Look for companies with margins minimally above 5%. Get excited when you see 15% and higher.

Filter #7: What's the Price to Sales Ratio? Anything above 10:1 isn't a good value, generally. Anything approaching 20:1 is likely nosebleed territory.

Filter #8: What is the Current Ratio? Look for at least a 2:1 ratio of Current Assets over Current Liabilities.

Filter #9: What is the Debt-to-Equity Ratio? I always feel more comfortable when this ratio is 25% or less. Above 50% is a red flag.

TOP DOWN CHECKLIST

What macro trends are favorable to your stock selection? For example, before I buy a semiconductor stock, I would ask myself– will there be more semiconductors in use five years from now or less? Before I buy a credit card stock, I would ask myself– will people use cash more or credit cards more five years from now? If I consider buying an oil stock, I would ask myself– will people use products that require more fossil fuels five years from now or less?

BUSINESS QUALITY CHECKLIST
1. Does it have a niche?
2. Do people have to keep buying it?
3. Can it keep competitors from copying the product and selling it at a lower price?
4. Does it have an Economic Moat? Patent? Network Effect?
5. Is it a Toll Road?
6. Is it Disruptive?
7. Is it a Category Killer?
8. Does it have low capital costs?
9. Does it scale?

Okay, I understand that answering all of these questions might seem like too much work and take the fun out of investing. But I strongly suggest answering most of these questions before you sink your hard-earned dollars into a stock. And if you challenge yourself and answer all of these questions, and actually do find a stock that meets all the criteria, you've got a good shot at being successful.

You're the Analyst: Always Keep Analyzing!

Remember, as a "Shark Investor," you didn't find your stock picks in magazines, hear them from CNBC gurus, or read them on *Reddit*. You picked the stocks– you're the analyst. As Peter Lynch said– and I'm paraphrasing– "Investing in stocks is like playing an endless game of 5-card stud." The game never ends– you'll always need to stay aware of what's happening with the businesses of your individual stock picks.

THE SHARK INVESTOR
YOU'RE THE ANALYST

With ETFs, you can set it and forget it. With individual stocks, you've got to stay trained on your investments.

If you own Lululemon, you should go to the mall and check out the foot traffic at the store. Are there shoppers? Are the store clerks busy engaging with customers or are they standing around? Look through the inventory. Get into a conversation with a store manager.

Before I bought Chipotle stock about 17 years ago, I frequented a Chipotle near my home in Boston, and made it a point to chat up the manager. I was surprised to learn that his store was the *only* Chipotle in New England. And the manager told me about the expansion plans. It wasn't "inside information." I was just hearing from the horse's mouth some of the information Chipotle disclosed in corporate filings. The line was always to the door at Chipotle, and I would compare it to the nearby Qdoba, which never seemed to be even ¼ full. It made me envision 50 or 100 Chipotles in New England (today there are 140).

If you own SNAP (Snapchat), ask your teenagers what social media apps they use. One New Year's Eve party I struck up a conversation with some teenage friends of my son. I asked them: "What apps are you using– are you using Facebook, Twitter?" No– Facebook and Twitter (X) were not so popular with this age group.

I kept hearing from the teenagers that they used Snapchat, Instagram, and TikTok. That gave me the confidence to double down on Snapchat when it was at $9.00 and unloved by Wall Street. This was before COVID. During COVID, Shapchat raced to $75.00, and I didn't sell a single share! Probably a mistake to have sold nothing during this parabolic move, but I decided to stick with the entrepreneur/ founder Evan Spiegel. Spiegel hasn't proven himself to be in the same league of visionaries as Jobs, Zuckerberg, and Ellison, but he did have the *cajones* to turn down a $3 billion offer from Facebook in 2013 when Snapchat was just two years old. My teenage daughter just recently told me she's in love with the Snapchat AI bot. She's thrilled with the bot's language functionality, which can speak to her in any language.

I'm going to ride the coattails of this entrepreneur– Spiegel– a little bit longer, and hope that he's able to successfully monetize his current 400 million users. I've checked again with my children and High School interns as to Snapchat's ubiquity with teenagers. The app is sticky. One of my interns says he uses the app "too much."

Teladoc was a stock I picked up prior to COVID. The company focuses on telehealth and the business model appeared fit for modern times. COVID of course seemed like the perfect accelerant for weaning patients off of clinical visits, and using technology for some examinations. Around this time my son had a knee injury playing soccer, and after the surgery we had a tele-visit with the surgeon. To my surprise, the telehealth visit was conducted via Zoom. After we talked with the surgeon, I asked the physician's assistant how come we weren't conducting our visit via a service like Teladoc. He replied that they had used another similar service, but that it didn't work very well. Interesting!

As COVID continued to limit direct, non-emergency contact with physicians, I had a couple of issues that required medical consultation. One of them was conducted simply using iPhone's Facetime, and the other was conducted via Epic Systems (the software company behind a significant number of medical organizations). I investigated Epic's telehealth offering and learned that it utilized a Zoom integration.

Confounded– I asked myself, where was Teladoc? Billed as the leader in medical tele-consultations, I didn't see them being utilized in any of my family's medical care. Recall my idea regarding investing in companies of which you are a customer. I had bought Teladoc stock without ever using the service. And then with the onset of COVID, I expected to start using the service. I had broken one of my cardinal rules in that I was not a customer. I was hoping to become a customer, but my medical experiences were not providing the opportunity.

It made me ask myself: "What are the real assets in telehealth?" And considering our family had medical consultations using Zoom and Face-time, I realized the *connectivity was not the asset.* As I mentioned in the section on "fake technology" companies, the assets are the doctors and medical staff– period. *How* you talk to them– land line, Zoom, Google, Facetime, etc.– is just an arbitrary conduit, and thus a commodity. From what I could see, Teladoc had no lock on speaking with doctors remote-ly. At the time I had this revelation, Teladoc stock was still riding the COVID high, and sported a market cap above $20 billion. I determined that Teladoc was not likely going to be a long-term winner. Having al-ready made 4-5x my investment, I decided to start taking profits.

As we'll discuss– determining when to sell and if one should ever sell– is a very difficult decision. But in this case, seeing the enormous upward move the stock had made during COVID, yet failing to see that its business model would gain long-term traction, the decision to sell was correct. As of this writing, Teladoc is about 90% off of its high set February of 2021.

The important point here is that you must be the analyst for your stocks– *before you pick them and after*. You must continually assess if your company is still the market leader you thought it was. Is the CEO who you thought was amazing when you picked the stock still at the helm? Is the earnings growth rate holding strong? Are competitors still finding it difficult to attack the space? In Jim Cramer's book *Real Mon-*

ey, the CNBC show host advises spending one hour per week doing "homework" *per* individual stock position. That means keeping up with news on the company, particularly the quarterly earnings reports. And if you don't have the time, Cramer declares you should be in an index fund. As Cramer articulates, it's not simply buy and hold, it's "buy and homework."

THE SHARK INVESTOR

PART VIII

HOW TO SELL STOCKS

INVESTMENT BOOKS TYPICALLY EXPLAIN HOW TO BUY STOCKS, but very few of them discuss strategies for selling. Astonishingly, there is very little written on the subject. Imagine the staggering volume of words produced on the buy part of the equation, but rare existence of advice on how to sell. And it takes both actions to successfully produce a profit.

I recently perused the investment section of a large Barnes and Noble bookstore and found a scant number of books, and even scarcer number of pages, devoted to selling stocks.

Peter Lynch devotes 11 pages of *One Up on Wall Street* to selling, and his 11 are some of the best written. Lynch focuses his selling tutorial on *types* of companies, such as when to sell a turnaround or a cyclical.

Jim Cramer's *Real Money,* offers the chapter "Spotting Tops," which offers sage advice for identifying market, corporate, and regulatory events that should trigger sell opportunities.

What I find is that most investors get tripped up on general price action– up or down– regardless of whether the company is a turnaround or a cyclical.

THE SHARK INVESTOR
HOW TO SELL STOCKS

And remember, the majority of investors who owned Fidelity's Magellan fund while Peter Lynch was the manager lost money. Clearly *buying* stocks, mutual funds, or ETFs is the easy part. The hard part is holding them and figuring out *when* and *if* ever to sell them. And if we sell stocks– in what proportion? Investor behavior– particularly around selling– is key. We learned this early on in the book when we discussed the *Kiplinger* magazine article on why fund managers underperform the S&P. And the point is buttressed when we consider the majority of investors lost money owning the greatest mutual fund in the world (Lynch's Magellan).

WHAT ARE WE LOOKING TO ACCOMPLISH WITH INDIVIDUAL STOCK SELECTION?

Many years ago– in one of my stock market classes, I spoke about Krispy Kreme as an example of a growth stock. Believe it or not, doughnut shop operator Krispy Kreme was a hot growth story in the early 2000s. As they would open a new store in a major market, the company's PR team would do a fabulous job of stirring local excitement, and by the time the doors finally opened, lines of salivating customers extended down the block. The stock moved quickly after its IPO debut, eventually peaking 135% above its IPO price.

A student approached me after the class and told me that he had bought Krispy Kreme stock at $25.00 and the stock was trading at $40.00. "Fantastic" I told him. He wasn't smiling though, and then proceeded to tell me he had sold the stock at $27.50. Now I understood the dour expression.

So, the question is– did the student make a good choice in selling Krispy Kreme when it was up 10% a few months after his purchase?

While 10% might have seemed like an acceptable gain, by selling *all* of his position, he missed out on the opportunity to double his money.

My first supposition is that a 10% gain is not a worthwhile target for an individual stock pick. Remember, the S&P 500 has averaged 10% a year for the last 90 years, and the QQQ ETF (see page 191) has averaged approximately 14.5% over the last 20 years. With returns like this available via diversified ETFs, why take the risk in owning an individual name and settle for 10%? If you're going to buy an individual name– at a minimum– think of making a return that exceeds the S&P 500.

Furthermore, the sections of this book covering individual stocks have not been about being average or even a little above average. We're "Sharks," and we want to achieve stellar returns; returns commensurate with the gains visionary entrepreneurs achieve with their companies. We won't end up as rich as Bezos, Zuckerberg, Knight (Nike CEO), or Hastings (Netflix CEO)– but we can own their stocks long term and capture annualized compounding returns of 20% and beyond.

But in order to do so, we must hold them long term. At the same time, we must be wary of "Nosebleed Valuations," parabolic moves, minor declines, dumpster fires, and other investment situations that may cause poor decision making. Let's explore some of these price movement variables investors inevitably encounter, and determine how to behave.

How to Sell Stocks When They Are Up

YOU'VE DOUBLED YOUR MONEY
Doubling one's money in the stock market is one of the great aspirations of all investors. Of course it begs the question, if you doubled your

money in a stock– how long did it take for you to double your money? If it took two years– that's pretty impressive. That means you got a 36% annualized return. If it took 10 years, it means you achieved a 7.2% return, and 7.2% is less than then S&P historical return of 9.8%. See the section on **"Rule of 72"** for an easy mathematical trick to determine how long it will take to double your money given a certain rate of return.

There is a "Rule" that gets bandied about known as the "Sell Half Rule," which suggests an investor sell half of a position once it doubles. The idea is you lock in profits, you get your principal returned, and now you are playing with the "house" money.

While this "rule" might appear to evince some wisdom, I would strongly advise against employing it. Selling after doubling one's money, without thinking about the underlying investment, can severely damage a potential game-changing stock. Here's an example:

Almost 10 years ago I invested $2,000 in NVIDIA. Of course I had never been a direct customer of NVIDIA, but had owned laptops that utilized their graphics chips. That's pretty much all I knew about the company– that they were a leader in graphics semiconductors. Adjusted for splits, my buy-in price was about 50 cents. Yes, you read that correctly. Within a couple of years the stock had doubled, and I decided to take half of my position off the table. This was before there was incessant talk of NVIDIA being the leading chip provider for powering Big Data, and no one was talking about Artificial Intelligence.

After the stock was up four-fold by 2016, I sold another 25% of my position.

Well, most of you realize this is a sad story to tell. Yes– I was locking in profits and had made a successful investment, but there was really no reason to take profits. The company was continuing to make headlines and eventually grew into the largest market cap semiconductor company, and then the 3rd largest U.S. market cap company by 2024.

All of the fundamentals would say hold this stock. Yet, I felt compelled to "lock-in" profits. I ended up making about 10x on my initial $2,000. But, if I had never sold a share, my position would have grown to approximately $450,000. I had purchased shares in one of the miraculous rocket ships we've discussed throughout this book. But I didn't have the discipline to just hold onto the shares like Warren Buffett or amateur investor Herbie Wertheim (whom we discussed earlier) would have done.

YOU'VE GOT A MEGA-WINNER

Let's imagine that you resisted the temptation to sell after doubling your money, and your stock has now quadrupled in value. THIS is where I would begin to consider taking some profits. Remember, you don't know if you've got an Amazon or a Blackberry, an NVIDIA or a Polaroid. Is it a company that keeps evolving and growing its earnings, or will the company get disrupted?

If you sell, sell gradually. At this juncture I would consider taking 5-15% off the table. The emphasis is consider. But the chief point to contemplate is: what do you know about the company? Is it continuing to grow earnings briskly? Does it still appear to be a leader in its space?

Be mindful that there is no exact science here, so by selling gradually, you avoid making a categorical decision (soon discussed). If you're up 4x and you sell 10% of your position, it means you've still got plenty of money on the table if the company continues to perform. At the same time, you've captured some profits in case things falter.

A recent CNBC article profiling Jay Chaudry, the billionaire CEO of

THE SHARK INVESTOR
HOW TO SELL STOCKS

Zscaler, buttresses this point. Chaudry's first startup, SecureIT, was acquired by VeriSign (Nasdaq:VRSN) for $70 million in VeriSign stock. Jim Bidzos, then the Chairman of VeriSign, provided Chaudry sage advice on what to do with his VeriSign shares: "Sell some of the stock little by little on a regular basis."

As Peter Lynch says, owning stocks is like playing an endless game of stud poker. You must continue to evaluate and assess your investment. How were the company's profits in its most recent earnings report? What is management saying about its business? And remember– you're the analyst! If you own Chipotle, do you still see long lines at your location? If you keep getting green signals, the longer you'll want to go without taking any profits. If you get yellow signals– earnings growth appears to be slowing, lines appear to be getting smaller, product innovation is stalling, etc.– then a gradual profit taking process can be accelerated.

YOU'VE GOT A BIG POSITION, A BIG PROFIT, AND THE HOLDING CONSTITUTES A BIG PART OF YOUR NET WORTH

If you've had the great fortune to work for a publicly traded company where over time you've developed a large position in the company's stock, establish a system that's automatic for gradually locking in profits and diversifying your position.

As an example, I had a friend who was part of a management team that sold a records keeping company to Iron Mountain (NYSE:IRM). He ended up with approximately $400K in Iron Mountain stock, which accounted for most of his net worth. He was largely bullish on Iron Mountain, but also wanted some liquidity. So, he developed a strategy to sell approximately 2.5% of his stock each quarter, no matter where shares were trading. In fact, this strategy is in tune with what you'll see most

CEOs employ. They will consistently sell a predetermined amount of stock at regular intervals.

If you are an employee of a firm where you've amassed a sizable holding, it's important not to fall in love with your company stock. In the 1990s I had a client at a long-forgotten, high-flying tech company called FTP Software. As one of the early employees, he attained around $1,000,000 in shares. He had sold $100K after the IPO, but was stubbornly holding onto the rest of the position. When FTP shares took a dive on an earnings miss, against my advice, he went into the open market to buy *more* shares thinking they had become a bargain. Unfortunately, there was no turnaround for FTP Software, and a once-millionaire saw his net worth plummet.

We saw a similar story with ENRON employees who held onto their shares with a nearly religious zeal. They believed that selling ENRON stock was somehow being traitorous, and many wealthy employees saw fortunes wiped out when Enron went bankrupt.

Repeat: don't fall in love with your company stock. If you've got a big position that comprises a significant portion of your net worth, establish a regular strategy for taking some money off the table each year if not quarterly.

Don't Make Categorical Decisions

Implicit in the advice on selling winners– but better stated explicitly– is don't make categorical decisions; that is: all or none.

This may seem like obviously intelligent wisdom, but you'd be surprised at how many folks tend to think in all or none terms.

THE SHARK INVESTOR
HOW TO SELL STOCKS

A relative of mine worked at JCPenney for most of her career, and when she retired, she held about $100,000 worth of Penney's stock. JCP shares (as they once traded on the NYSE) had experienced a pretty good ride coinciding with her retirement, and so she decided it would be a good time to sell– *all of her shares*. So, she sold in the low seventies, and of course soon after selling, the shares briskly moved to a little above $100.00. Feeling annoyed that she had sold her shares at such a low price, this relative decided to buy shares at $100.00, and get back on the Penney's train. And of course, just shortly after she purchased at $100.00, Penney's earnings stumbled and shares plummeted.

Time and time again I hear investors say that they don't want to sell a position because they are afraid of losing out if it goes up. They make an unnecessary all or none call. If you have accumulated a large position in a security, and you're ready to take some off the table– do it. Take 10% or 25%. If the stock goes up, take another take 10% or 25%. It's the same exercise we discussed in "You've Got a Winner." Take some profits and leave more on the table.

This same relative had a nice position in Apple due to a recommendation I gave her in 2002. However, in the throes of the financial crisis of 2009, she got depressed over her slumping Apple shares and sold *all of her shares* (against my advice). If she had held the shares until 2015, she would have created a multi-hundred thousand dollar position. If she felt compelled to sell some of them in the pit of the Financial Crisis, so be it. Just 1/3 of her position would have been worth 100K by 2015. But it was all or none for her.

What to Do When a Stock is Down?

THE STOCK IS DOWN SLIGHTLY AND EVERY REASON
YOU BOUGHT THE STOCK STILL EXISTS

As we'll discuss in "Stern's Laws," soon after you buy a company's stock, there's a good chance the shares will decline. It's just one of those strange investment ironies. Maybe a war breaks out. Maybe there's a terrorist attack. Maybe a competing company in the space reports poor earnings. None of these events are specific to your company. If exogenous factors catalyze a fall in the share price of one of your holdings, it could be an opportunity to buy more.

Over a decade ago I invested in Baidu, often called the "Google of China." Within a month of buying Baidu, shares were down nearly 20% on no specific news. There wasn't a poor earnings report or any issuance of negative guidance. There was simply a general market malaise. All of the reasons why I bought Baidu initially still existed, so I bought more shares– only this time I was getting an even better price. I then rode the shares up for a 10-bagger.

THE STOCK IS DOWN AND MOST OF THE REASONS WHY
YOU BOUGHT THE STOCK HAVE CHANGED

Before you buy shares in a company, you should have a story that details the specific reasons why the shares are a compelling buy: strong management, great products, an economic moat, fast earnings growth, etc. But what if the story changes? What if a year into your holding, the Founder/CEO leaves the company. A new disruptive technology is putting pressure on earnings. The company had been debt free, but now is taking on debt to acquire a company and the acquisition seems illogical.

THE SHARK INVESTOR
HOW TO SELL STOCKS

Once again– *you're the Analyst*, and you're going to need to make the call. If most of the reasons why you bought the company have changed, it could be a good time to sell. You don't have to exit the entire position. Just as we discussed earlier in "Categorical Decisions," don't make one. But it's probably a good time to take some money off the table and watch the company very closely. If management doesn't indicate a strong turn-around story, it could be time to accelerate your sell orders.

There is no exact science, and that's why I recommend not making a categorical decision and dumping all of your shares when things look bleak. Lululemon (Nasdaq:LULU) initially experienced torrid growth with its founding CEO, then went through two management shakeups, product controversies, and lackluster performance before settling on its current CEO, who has led the company to higher highs.

THE STOCK IS DOWN SUBSTANTIALLY FROM YOUR PUR-CHASE PRICE

Unfortunately, research into behavioral finance indicates that investors are very quick to take profits but tend to hold onto their losers. The opposite behavior would be more effective. If you've got a so-called "Fallen Angel," a stock that has dropped significantly from your purchase price, you should take action.

GoPro was a hot brand when it went public in 2014 and its shares quickly rallied from the offer price of $24.00 to a high above $90.00. Unfortunately, the company squandered a good deal of its IPO proceeds trying to build its own media production division, growth stalled, and shares today flounder in the $2.00 range.

Ladies and gentlemen– if you are one of the unlucky investors who purchased GoPro shares around the IPO price, or god forbid at the zenith nosebleed price of $93.00, it's time to sell. Read on about the benefits of selling your "Dumpster Fires."

Don't Be Afraid To Sell Your Dumpster Fires

In a landmark behavioral finance study, University of California professors Brad Barber and Terrance Odean found that investor behavior often stands in the way of successful investing. Their research uncovered a strong "Disposition Effect;" that is the tendency for investors to sell winners quickly and hold onto losers.

While it is possible that a laggard eventually turns into a winner (which we'll discuss soon), I have found countless investors that will interminably hold onto securities that have lost 60% to 90% of their value.

I believe the psychology behind an investor's inertia is that the loss is only on paper when a security declines. If they sell a winner quickly, they can give themselves a pat on the back for making and taking a profit. But when they sell and recognize a loss, it feels like a slap in the face.

I will often hear investors explain they will sell a fallen stock when it rebounds to some level they have imagined. So, if they bought a stock at $90.00 and it's now at $10.00 they say: "Well, I'm going to sell it when it gets to $50.00"– a

number that is often randomly plucked. They seem naively unaware that a quintupling of the stock– moving from $10.00 to $50.00–requires a substantial change in business fortunes; that all the factors that pushed the stock down 80+% are reversed.

This is of course not impossible– witness stocks like Amazon and eBay–that were beaten down in the Dot Com bust. They recovered and went on to reach new highs.

But by taking action on a losing stock, there is a win-win. If you remain thoroughly bullish and are convinced your "Fallen Angel" will rise from the ashes and regain its former high-flying status, *sell it anyway*.

Capture the capital loss, write it off on your tax return, but buy it back 31 days later. And then you can hope that your calculation of long-term growth for the company comes to fruition. By waiting more than 30 days, an investor avoids the SEC's Wash-Sale rule, prohibiting the claim of a tax-loss if a security is repurchased within 30 days. Long-term losses can be written off against long-term capital gains. Short-term losses can be written off against short-term gains. If there are no gains, up to $3,000 can be written off annually against personal income, with carry forwards to future annual tax filings.

What's The Lesson of Blackberry?

Anyone above the age of forty reading this book is probably very familiar with the brand BlackBerry. The Canadian company Research in Motion, was one of the early developers of wireless technology, and sold devices under the name BlackBerry. Their phones, which could send and receive email, became ubiquitous in the early and mid 2000s. The company's stock, which listed on the Nasdaq in 1999, finished its first trading day at $1.92. By 2008, shares had climbed to a glorious perch of $139.00. This was a lovely nine-year run for investors, but unfortunately Steve Jobs decided to see if Apple could make inroads in the mobile phone space with its touch screen powered iPhone. Do we know the story from here? BlackBerry continued to manufacture their comparatively clunky keyboard driven device, and the stock price fell about as fast as it went up.

This is the investors' great paradox. Do you own a Blackberry or an Apple? And if you own an Apple, will your Apple someday become a Blackberry? There is no crystal ball to provide an answer. Disruptors eventually get disrupted. This is why we must repeat Peter Lynch's advice that: "Keeping up with a company in which you own stock is like playing an endless stud-poker hand."

You never can stop evaluating a company– you must be a permanent analyst as long as you own shares. BlackBerry, Cabletron, Cisco are just a few of the long list of companies that possessed all the qualities you would seek in a growth stock, and were spectacular investments– *for a period of time*. But unfortunately, they didn't make for *permanent* holdings. Finding the exact inflection point at which to aggressively sell shares will be impossible. You will need to stay abreast of the company's news, gather information about the industry they play in, and continue to assess future prospects. And follow the advice from the book section: "You've got a Mega-Winner."

The Stock is a Laggard

Let's define a laggard as a stock pick you've made that isn't keeping up with the market over a period of two to three years. So, this is distinct from buying a stock and in the same year, it happens to decline. A laggard may be a company that had strong earnings growth for a number of years but hits a rough patch that depresses shares relative to the market. Let's also define laggard, for our purposes, as a stock that is down 10% to 50%. If it's down more than 50%, you should probably look at the ideas under "Dumpster Fire."

Remember, the data shows that categorically selling your worst performers may be a negative. That's what we uncovered early in the book when we looked at why portfolio managers underperform the S&P. They jettison their winners too early and they let go of their laggards too early.

When determining whether you should retain a laggard, you should first ask yourself the same questions we'd ask for a short-term decliner: has anything changed significantly with the company? Did they report an accounting fraud? Did the longtime CEO get fired? Did a new competitor emerge that's gobbling up market share? If the answer is *no* to these types of questions, and all of the reasons you bought the stock still exist, then stay patient.

And even if a company is facing competitive headwinds, change is the driving force of corporate America. Companies change CEOs if the current CEO isn't the right fit. Steve Ballmer led Microsoft as CEO for approximately 14 years, and for 14 years the stock did nothing. As soon as Satya Nadella was named CEO in 2014, the stock went on a tear. It's up 10-fold after being dormant for more than a decade. In fact, as of this writing, it has surpassed Apple as the largest market cap company.

Companies change strategies when they encounter rough patches. A remarkable example is Garmin, the navigation technology company whose stock ran up tenfold in the early 2000s as every automobile driver installed a navigation device on their dashboard. Just when things couldn't look rosier, smartphones hit the market with the exact same chip set used in Garmin devices. Why pay for a Garmin when GPS is already available as an app on your phone? The stock plummeted and Garmin had to shift course, changing focus from auto GPS devices to wearables. Now they are a leader in smart watches and the stock has surpassed its 2007 high.

And if management can't figure it out on their own, stalled companies often attract the attention of activist investors. These Wall Street professionals– like Carl Icahn, Nelson Peltz, and Bill Ackman– target companies they feel aren't living up to their potential. They push for restructurings, CEO replacements, board changes, or even a complete sale of the company. They are often unwelcomed by the existing management, but their involvement often serves as a catalyst for changes that push their target stocks higher.

Remember– stocks and companies rarely follow linear progressions. When a company stalls, it's often smarter to keep at least some money on the table. Either existing management or activists often find ways to reignite the shares.

Determining a "Nosebleed Valuation"

When mountain climbers ascend peaks, they often experience nosebleeds at these nerve-wracking high altitudes. When a stock climbs to an

THE SHARK INVESTOR
HOW TO SELL STOCKS

unprecedented level disconnected from traditional valuation methods, we can employ the term "nosebleed." "Nosebleed Valuations" were the fashion in the 1960s with a set of growth stocks known as the "Nifty-Fifty;" in the late 1990s and early 2000s with the Dot Com bubble; and most recently during COVID, when many companies saw their valuations skyrocket in 6 to 12 months.

Some stocks are simply just too damn expensive. You might encounter companies that fulfill many of the criteria that we've discussed. The business model may be superb, they may have an amazing CEO, there could be incredible demand for the product, but Wall Street and investors have already deduced this– and have pushed the share price up so high that any buyer with a modicum of respect for proper valuation, must shy away from it.

This type of situation is often referred to as "Good company/ Bad stock." The company is amazing, but the price is preposterously too high.

But how do you actually separate a stock that's performing well and has a reasonable valuation from one you should get nervous about and avoid like the plague; or if you own the stock– think about aggressively selling shares?

"Nosebleed Valuations" might develop slowly over time, right at an IPO, or build rapidly when a mania develops over a group of stocks. In the Dot Com era, stocks with no earnings and scant revenues climbed to multi-billion dollar valuations. Traditional valuation metrics, such as P/E and PEG, were replaced with "eyeballs" and "clicks."

A recent example of a "Nosebleed Valuation" is Trump Media & Technology Group, with the trading symbol DJT. Yes– you got it right– this is Donald Trump's holding company for his "Truth Social" media platform.

174 **Part VIII**

THE SHARK INVESTOR
HOW TO SELL STOCKS

At the time of this writing, the operation is trading at a nearly $10 billion valuation. However, the company brought in about $5 million in revenue for all of 2023 while posting a nearly $50 million loss.

Investors appear to be buying the stock out of loyalty to Mr. Trump, and not concerned that they are paying 2,000 times existing revenues! While Mr. Trump is certainly idolized by his base, it's hard to argue that as a business, Trump Media is worth $10 billion.

Another well-known company that traded at a nosebleed valuation at its IPO is electric vehicle maker, Rivian Automotive (Nasdaq:RIVN).

Rivian went public in November of 2021 during the throes of the Meme stock mania. With an offering price of $78.00, investors bestowed the company with $12 billion of fresh capital, valuing the upstart at a whopping $66.5 billion.

Even though Rivian had just started shipping vehicles, shares opened at $106.75, and then soared to an intraday high of nearly $180.00. At that zenith, Rivian's market cap was a colossally gargantuan $150 billion!

How do we know this is a "Nosebleed Valuation"? Well, let's repeat that the company had barely shipped a vehicle, had scant revenues, and was projected to deliver billions in losses. How about we add on that Rivian's market cap (at its zenith) exceeded the combined market caps of Ford and General Motors, who together produce 10 million+ vehicles and sport revenues of $350 billion.

There's a sucker born every minute and a lot of them showed up for this display of irrational exuberance at Rivian's IPO. And where are RIVN shares today? Floundering around $12.00, at a still generous market cap of $11 billion.

Even if Rivian had revenues of $1 billion at the time of its IPO, it would have possessed a Price to Sales ratio of 150:1 at the peak. This is a nosebleed.

Software maker Snowflake (NYSE:SNOW) is another good example of a nosebleed stock. The company came public in September of 2020 raising $3.4 billion.

The Snowflake IPO price was set at $120.00 but rocketed to $275.00 within minutes of trading. Shares closed at $253.93, awarding the company a valuation of over $70 billion.

In its fiscal year ending January 31, 2019, Snowflake had revenue of $96.7 million. A year later that number was $264.7 million. This latter figure was delivered *after* the IPO, so even if investors were impressed with Snowflake's revenue growth and anticipated annual revenues in excess of $260 million, at the IPO price they were paying 240x these forward revenues.

And if 240x revenue sounds high, within a couple of weeks, Snowflake shares soared to $387.00, pushing its market cap to $90 billion (346x future sales). And today, Snowflake shares have fallen as snowflakes do, trading around $115.00.

Why NVIDIA is Not a Nosebleed

Not every stock that has a monster rally is necessarily a nosebleed. One might think that NVIDIA, whose shares rallied from $11.20 in mid-October of 2022 to above $90.00 by March of 2024, is the epitome of a nosebleed stock. Its chart looks like the left side of a parabola. But let's examine what propelled the shares: soaring revenue and earnings growth. Unlike Rivian, NVIDIA possessed the underlying fundamentals to justify its staggering price run to a $3 trillion market cap and the 3rd largest U.S. valuation.

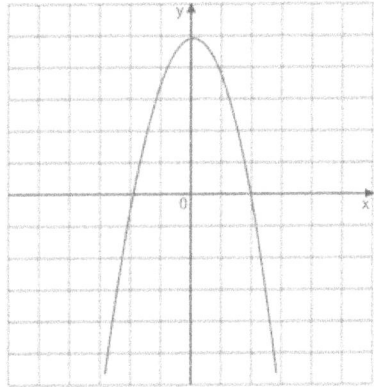

For its quarter ended January 28th of 2024, NVIDIA's revenue increased 265% from the year prior. And earnings were up 765% from 2023. While a $3 trillion valuation seems lofty for a company with $60 billion in revenues (50x sales), we must dig deeper and look at NVIDIA's Profit Margin. This is not your average S&P 500 company, with margins sitting around 11%. For Q4 of 2024, NVIDIA margins came in at just under 58%, a staggering figure.

Looking forward to the next 12 months, analysts see NVIDIA recording revenues above $100 billion, which means NVIDIA could comfortably post earnings of $50 billion. So, a current valuation of around $2.5 trillion is only 50x the earnings estimate for 2025, imputing a PEG ratio of 1.2. We won't say that NVIDIA is a bargain, but it's nothing like a Snowflake or Rivian.

Last Word on Nosebleeds

Keep in mind, if you're thinking about investing in a company sporting a nosebleed valuation, possessing a sky-high price doesn't make it a bad *company*, it just makes it un-investable for the present. If you're thinking about getting in– wait– and you'll likely see a significant correction to a more rational price.

If you own the shares– even though you may think of it as a long-term hold– you should consider accelerating your sales.

When shares hit a nosebleed level, they might have the next 10 years of optimistic growth (if it ever materializes) already built into the current stock price.

Classic nosebleed stock charts often resemble the geometric shape known as the parabola (see figure on previous page), often climbing in a nearly straight vertical. However, once the momentum dissipates– a poor earnings quarter is released, or other unexpected bad news materializes– the stock reacts with a corresponding quick downturn.

Indicators of the Likelihood of a "Nosebleed Valuation"

MARKET CAP EXCEEDS 20X SALES
An example would be a company with $1 billion in revenue trading with a $21 billion market cap (or higher).

PEG IS 5 OR ABOVE
An example would be company with a PE of 100 and an expected earnings growth rate of 20% per annum.

PART IX

GENERAL INVESTING

HOW MUCH MONEY SHOULD WE ALLOCATE TO STOCKS? There is no absolute right or wrong answer, but there is a handy formula to use.

Start with your age, and that figure minus 10, would equal the percentage of funds that should be allocated to fixed investments (such as CDs and bonds).

And it's always a good idea to have around 3-5% allocated to cash (savings or money market).

So, a 50-year-old might want to allocate 40% fixed, 5% cash, and the remaining 55% to stocks. If you're 80 years of age, a reasonable allocation would consist of 70% fixed investments, 25% equities, and 5% cash.

The precise cash position (of course) is a personal decision, but most advisors recommend having at least six months of living expenses set aside for emergencies. There is certainly nothing wrong with having twelve months of expenses set aside.

And by cash, we're not talking about a savings account earning nothing. A money market fund, which as of this writing is typically yielding 4.5%, is perfectly sufficient. It offers liquidity, reasonable safety (many are FDIC insured), and a healthy return.

When you develop your allocation plan, stick with it. Don't bounce around. Don't get excited about stocks or depressed about stocks and throw money in and out of the market. Remember it's not *timing* the market that counts. It's *time in* the market that's important (see "Should I Try And Time the Market?").

Model Equity Portfolio

So, let's say you're a 50-year-old with $500,000 in investable assets. You should have about 40% of your assets in fixed investments. If that's too conservative for your taste, you could look at 30%, but I wouldn't go much lower than that figure.

For our purposes here, if we stick with the 40% in fixed, and we look at 5% in cash, that would leave us 55% for equities– translating to 275K.

Of this 275K equity allocation, I would have 80-90% of it invested in equity ETFs. Yes, you heard me! While this book is largely about picking individual stocks, as we have demonstrated, the data shows just how perilous picking individual stocks can be.

While we are going to try and beat the market averages, we should proceed with great humility. The professionals rarely do it, so let's not assume we're going to be wildly successful either. And remember, an investment like the Qs (QQQ) is an ETF that has trounced the S&P 500 (see page 191). With an ETF like the Q's available, we can drive Alpha (S&P outperformance) with a lower-risk, diversified ETF.

But thanks to this book, we've learned some helpful pointers for picking an out-of-the-park, home run winner that turns out to be the next

Facebook, NVIDIA, Starbucks, Chipotle, etc.– and potentially makes us a small or even large fortune.

If 85% of our $275K equity portfolio is devoted to equity ETFs, that would leave us $41,250 for individual stocks. Let's just call it 40K to keep it simple.

With 40K allocated to individual stocks, we could consider 2K allocated to 20 different stocks, or 4K allocated to 10 stocks. This could be personal preference, although research cited by Burton Malkiel in his *A Random Walk Down Wall Street* suggests a portfolio of 60 stocks is statistically helpful for building a diverse portfolio. Twenty stock picks obviously offers more diversification than ten.

You don't have to make all your picks at the same time! You'll want to focus on well-researched positions that have met all or most of the criteria we have discussed. Maybe you'll find three companies a year that titillate your interest and meet your stringent due diligence standards.

Keep your bets relatively even. You don't know which one will be the winner!

Be patient. Only sell if you have good reason to believe there is no chance for the company to be successful. This is determined by information and data, not just getting discouraged because the stock is down or lagging.

Let's take a look at what a theoretical portfolio of individual stocks might look like in terms of projected returns after four years.

Let's narrow the portfolio down to 10 individual stock picks on which we have performed significant due diligence. We utilized our "Shark" instincts and selected 10 companies that meet our criteria of fast-growing, entrepreneur-led companies, and we know and love their products.

Stock #1 knocks it out of the park and is up 5x after four years. We have an additional pick (#2) that increases 15% per annum for four years. Our next six stocks return 10% per annum, in line with the S&P 500.

Our ninth stock does absolutely nothing after four years, and our tenth stock is a real dog, declining by 50%.

If you take a look at the chart below, you can see that our returns are pretty good overall; in fact– they beat the historical return of the market. Our portfolio would be up 70% after four years, sporting a 14.24% annualized return.

STOCK	START	RESULT	1	2	3	4
1	$2,000	5x return	$2,990	$4,770	$6,682	$10,000
2	$2,000	+15%	$2,300	$2,645	$3,041	$3,498
3	$2,000	+10%	$2,200	$2,420	$2,662	$2,928
4	$2,000	+10%	$2,200	$2,420	$2,662	$2,928
5	$2,000	+10%	$2,200	$2,420	$2,662	$2,928
6	$2,000	+10%	$2,200	$2,420	$2,662	$2,928
7	$2,000	+10%	$2,200	$2,420	$2,662	$2,928
8	$2,000	+10%	$2,300	$2,420	$2,662	$2,928
9	$2,000	Nothing	$2,000	$2,000	$2,000	$2,000
10	$2,000	Loses 50%	$1,500	$1,250	$1,100	$1,000
	$20,000					$34,066

Even if you employ the principles in this book, you will pick dog stocks. And you will also pick stocks that simply keep in line with market averages. However, if one of your picks is a winner, it can make up for the laggards in the portfolio. But remember, you'll need to be patient. If you sell stock #1, the big winner after it is up 15%, you'll never see its gargantuan growth materialize.

The Rule of 72

If a company's earnings per share grow at 24% a year– how long will it take for EPS to double? The answer: 3 years.

If I earn 6% on a Treasury Bond, how long will it take to double my money? The answer: 12 years.

How am I deriving these answers? From a simple arithmetic "trick" called the Rule of 72. Not mathematically perfect (but close enough), the Rule of 72 allows you to rapidly determine the basic number of years it will take for you to double your investment (given a rate of return).

Take the percentage return (of any investment) and divide that figure

Annual Interest Rate	The Rule of 72	Actual Number of Years
1%	72.00	69.66
2%	36.00	35.00
3%	24.00	23.45
4%	18.00	17.67
5%	14.40	14.21
10%	7.2	7.27
20%	3.6	3.8
30%	2.4	2.64
50%	1.44	1.71
75%	.96	1.24
100%	.72	1.00

into 72. A company's stock is forecasted to grow 12% each year. How long will it take for it to double? Divide 12 into 72, and presto– it will take 6 years for the stock to double.

You've been earning 18% in your 401(k) each year? Divide 18 into 72, and *voila*– it will take 4 years for your savings to double.

If a Series EE bond is guaranteed to double in 20 years, what is the implied rate of return? Divide 20 into 72 and you get 3.6%.

If you look at the chart (previous page), you can see that the Rule of 72 loses its magic once it gets past 30%. Obviously if you earn 100% on your investment, it will take 1 year to double, not .72.

This trick can be handy when you are looking at an investment statement. If your investment adviser brags to you that his recommendations doubled your money, you better check to see how long it took for he/she to make it happen. If it took four years, they generated 18% per annum in your portfolio. However, if it took 18 years to double your money, they were generating only a 4% return.

What is an ETF?

Much like a mutual fund, an exchange-traded fund– or ETF– is a basket of securities. However, unlike a mutual fund, which is purchased and redeemed directly with the mutual fund company, an ETF is bought and sold through a brokerage firm on a stock exchange. ETFs are utilized for the same reasons an investor utilizes a mutual fund: to gain diversification and professional management.

Investing in ETFs combines the flexibility of trading individual stocks with the built-in diversification of mutual funds.

There *are* index-focused mutual funds such as Vanguard's 500 Index fund (VFIAX). However, the majority of equity mutual funds are *actively* managed. That is, there is a fund manager exerting their particular opinion as to what are good and bad stocks to own, and what are good and bad times to be invested. Active managers also make decisions on when to take profits and when to cut losses.

ETFs on the other hand, typically simulate the performance of an index. There is professional management, but they don't make buy and sell decisions based on their personal opinion of equities. If company ABC is listed in the S&P 500 index, and an ETF tracks the S&P 500, then the ETF manager's job is to buy and hold ABC company for as long as it is part of the index.

There are ETFs following indexes for the S&P 500, Mid Cap stocks, and Russell 2000 (Small Caps). They also exist for international stocks and sectors (like banks, biotech, and real estate). You can also buy ETFs for bonds, currencies, and commodities.

ETFs Versus Mutual Funds: Which One is the Champ?

TRADING

ETFs: Trade throughout the day like stocks, so the price fluctuates constantly. You can buy or sell at any point during trading hours. If you buy at 10:00 am, you get the 10:00 am price.

Mutual Funds: Can be bought or sold throughout the trading day, but the price you receive is the 4:00 pm *closing* price. If you wake up one morning and decide to buy an S&P 500 mutual fund at 10:00am, you get the 4:00 pm closing price.

MANAGEMENT

ETFs: Mostly are passively managed, meaning they track an index and don't require a fund manager to constantly pick securities.

Mutual Funds: Can be actively or passively managed. Actively managed funds have a manager who tries to outperform the market, while passively managed funds track an index (similar to most ETFs).

INVESTMENT MINIMUMS

ETFs: ETFs do not have minimum investments. If one share of Vanguard's Growth ETF (VUG) costs $345.00, that's all you need to get in the game.

Mutual Funds: Conversely, mutual funds often require minimums ranging from $500.00 to several thousand dollars. Vanguard's retirement funds require a $1,000.00 minimum, their actively managed funds $3,000.00, and their Admiral series have minimums ranging from

Mutual Funds

ETFs

$3,000.00 to $100,000.00.

TAX EFFICIENCY
ETFs: Generally, more tax-efficient because the passive index strategy keeps portfolio turnover low, minimizing capital gains distributions.

Mutual Funds: May distribute capital gains more frequently depending on the fund's trading activity.

TRANSPARENCY
ETFs: Must disclose their holdings each day.

Mutual Funds: Report their holdings only quarterly, and there is generally a time lag between the end of the quarter and the publication of the holdings.

FEES
ETFs: Typical annual management expenses range from just a few basis points to 50 basis points (1/2 of a percent). As an example, the Vanguard S&P 500 ETF (VOO) has an annual management fee of .03%.

Mutual Funds: Typical expenses range from 1/2 of a percent to 1.5%.

THE TITLE FIGHT: ETFs vs. Mutual Funds
ETFs offer more trading flexibility and precision

ETFs provide more transparency

ETFs are more tax efficient than mutual funds
ETFs often have lower fees and expenses

ETFs do not require minimum investment amounts

ETFs generally follow passive investment strategies mimicking an index

THE WINNER: ETFs!

How Can I Find ETFs?

The growth of ETFs from 2003 to 2022 is nothing short of staggering. According to research from Statista, there were 8,754 ETFs globally in 2022, compared to 276 in 2003. As you might imagine, the largest ETFs are those tracking the S&P 500.

The original fund in this space, the SPDR (often pronounced as "spider"), is the big daddy with approximately $563 billion under management, and the next eight big ETFs are all equity funds. When we get to the 10th largest, we find our first bond ETF. Vanguard is a big player in the ETF space, holding 5 of the top 10 positions. And they probably offer the lowest cost family of both equity and bond ETFs available. The Vanguard S&P 500 ETF (VOO) as well as its Total Stock Market ETF (VTI) can both be owned with a total annual management cost of .03%. Compare this figure of 3 tenths of a percent with many mutual funds charging a management fee of 1%. And the actively managed funds often deliver lousy performance to boot!

Don't forget, there are ETFs for nearly every discipline of investing. An investor can find an ETF for owning stocks in Egypt or Greece. There are ETFs for commodities like soybeans and copper; currencies like the Yen or Swiss Franc; and even funds that make bets on market volatility.

The average investor doesn't need to worry about investing in soybeans and copper. In fact, I would recommend avoiding investing in these spaces unless you have a particular need.

But I do recommend taking a look at a free ETF Database from VettaFi at etfdb.com. Click on Screener and you'll be able to sort through more than 3,400 ETFs ranging from basic equity and bond funds to exotic ETFs focused on hedge funds or managed futures. You can utilize filters for ESG (Environmental/Social/Governance) scores or Dividend Yields, and much more.

Once again, you won't need to dabble in exotic strategies. The average investor can probably live with 4-10 equity ETFs. But poking around at etfdb.com can certainly be edifying for any investor. And certainly, if you have an ESG preference, browsing etfdb.com can be invaluable.

Can I Buy a Fund that Owns the S&P 500?

With all this talk about the amazing returns of the S&P 500 over the last 90 years– and the incapacity for most active fund managers to match the index's results– can you buy a fund that just owns the S&P 500?

Hallelujah– yes you can!

S&P 500 Index funds seek to replicate the performance of the index by investing in S&P 500 companies with similar weights. So, if Apple's market cap (and Apple currently has one of the largest market caps) makes up 6.35% of the S&P 500, the fund will apportion 6.35% of its assets to owning Apple shares.

These funds employ a passive or indexing investment strategy, and will only make changes in the portfolio if the index changes its positions (which rarely happens). So, if Tesla gets added to the S&P 500, then fund managers following the index will buy Tesla shares in proportion to Tesla's market cap.

Thus, these funds provide the average individual investor the capacity to own the index and participate in the growth of the 500 largest U.S. companies by market cap, and essentially make a bet on the success of American capitalism. This is a simple decision– you buy and hold the index– and the professional fund manager does the rest of the work.

Another thing– the expense ratio on these index funds is generally very, very low. Another benefit.

There are both Mutual Funds and ETFs that mimic the S&P 500.

Some of the largest S&P 500 mutual funds include:
Vanguard 500 Index Fund Admiral Shares (VFIAX)
Fidelity 500 Index Fund (FXAIX)

The largest ETFs that own the S&P 500 include:
SPDR S&P 500 ETF Trust (SPY)
iShares Core S&P 500 ETF (IVV)
Vanguard S&P 500 ETF (VOO)

Is the S&P 500 a High Bar?

We've discussed the S&P 500 quite a lot in this book, and for very good reason: it's the main index used to measure stock market performance, as well as to benchmark the performance of investment managers. A manager may tout excellent performance– but compared to what? The S&P acts as an easy yardstick for determining relative performance.

The S&P 500, of course, is comprised of 500 stocks: U.S. headquartered, publicly-traded companies that generally possess market caps of $10 billion and above.

What about the other U.S. headquartered, publicly-traded companies that are smaller than the top 500? There are thousands of other companies listed on the Nasdaq and NYSE. They deserve some attention as well, don't they?

With all the talk about the S&P 500– and the mega-cap names like NVIDIA, Tesla, Microsoft, Amazon, Apple, Meta, and Google– you'd think that all of these other companies were– as Gordon Gekko says in the movie "Wall Street"– "dogs with fleas." But it would be a mistake to assume that all of the action is in the biggest names, and that these thousands of smaller to medium sized companies should be ignored.

WHAT ABOUT MID CAPS? THEY HAVE DESTROYED LARGE CAPS OVER THE LAST 25 YEARS

Mid Caps are generally thought of as companies with market capitalizations between $2 and $10 billion. According to State Street, since 1994 Mid Caps have outperformed Large Caps 52.9% of the time and Small Caps 50.4%. There are several indexes that follow Mid Caps including the CRSP U.S. Mid Cap Index, the Russell MidCap Index, the Dow Jones U.S. Mid-Cap Total Stock Market Index, and the S&P MidCap 400 Index. And then there are dozens of ETFs that track these indexes.

Take a look the table below. While large caps have outperformed their smaller cousins over the last 10 years, study the 25-year return for Mid Caps. It's absolutely stunning that not only did Mid Caps outperform Large Caps, but absolutely walloped them, more than doubling their performance!

WHAT ABOUT SMALL CAPS? THEY HAVE OUTPACED LARGE CAPS OVER 65 YEARS

And even lower on the stock food chain sit Small Caps, usually considered to be companies with market valuations beneath $2 billion.

According to an analysis of foreign and U.S. investments from De-

Trailing 10 Year Total Return	2013-2023
Large Cap Stocks	+ 162%
Mid Cap Stocks	+ 139%
Small Cap Stocks	+ 108%
Trailing 25 Year Return	**1998-2023**
Mid Cap Stocks	+ 639%
Small Cap Stocks	+ 310%
Large Cap Stocks	+ 278%
Source: Bloomberg Data: Large Cap S&P 500;	S&P MidCap 400; Small Cap Russell 2000

cember 1998 through June 2023, researchers at index provider MSCI found that Small Cap stocks outperformed large firms over 15-year periods about 9 in 10 times.

Examining a longer historical time frame, Wharton professor Jeremy Siegel, in his essential book *Stocks for the Long Run*, notes that from 1926-2021 Small Cap stocks earned an average annualized return of 11.99% vs. the S&P's 10.35%. From 1975 to 1983 the battle between Small Caps and Large Caps wasn't even close, with Small Caps delivering a 35.3% compound annual return vs. 15.7% for Large Caps.

Firms such as S&P, MSCI, and Russell maintain indexes of Small Cap stocks, and there are multiple investment management firms– Vanguard, Invesco, Fidelity– offering ETFs that seek to mimic the respective index's return.

iShares' Core S&P Small-Cap ETF tracks a narrower group of 680 Small Cap stocks; whereas the iShares Russell 2000 ETF tracks 1,969 Small Cap stocks. Vanguard's Small Cap ETF tracks 1,422 companies. Invesco has several different Small Cap ETFs filtering for quality, growth, momentum, and revenue.

As you can see, the possibility for variations on Small Cap ETFs, or any index for that matter, can continue *ad infinitum*. Anyone can create an index ETF and apply different filters. They are managed passively, but have specific criteria affecting the composition.

The Simplest Equity Investment You Can Make

If your ETF head is spinning between Large Cap, Mid Cap, Small Cap; S&P, MSCI, Russell; Vanguard, iShares, Invesco– and you're screaming "I can't take it, could someone recommend one simple investment?"

Yes– in fact with one fund you can own the entire U.S. stock market! From the biggest Mega Caps down to the Micro Caps, Vanguard's Total Market Index (VTI) contains 3,761 stocks.

By utilizing this single strategy, you don't need to be a slave to the endless analysis of ETFs. Are Large Caps the place to be? But what about Mid Cap Growth names? Or what about Small Cap Value stocks?

The endless stock rumination can be put to rest, and with a single holding, you've got the entire market. In Vanguard's Total Market Index ETF, all of the stocks are held in proportion to their market caps. A company like Apple, with a $3 trillion dollar valuation, constitutes about 6.00% of the fund; Costco, with a market cap of around $400 billion, comprises .68% of the fund; and so on down the list, with many of the stocks so small they don't even register within two decimal points.

With a Total Market Fund, if Big Cap stocks do well, you own them; if Small Cap stocks put in a strong decade of performance– fantastic– you own them; if Mid Caps have another marvelous period, you own them as well.

You own the entire market: Value, Growth; Big, Medium, and Small. You won't need a Large Cap Value fund, and a Mid Cap Growth fund, and a Small Cap Value fund, etc. All of the tiers of market capitalization are included in one fund. All the stocks are owned proportionally relative to their size in the market.

Winners with rising market caps will rise to the top and constitute a larger percentage of the overall fund. Losers will sink and constitute a smaller part of the index portfolio.

And all you need to do is make one buy.

The Vanguard Total Market fund is such a singular, comprehensive investment, Vanguard's own employees are NOT offered an S&P 500 fund in the company's 401(k) plan. According to an article at *MarketWatch*, Vanguard removed the S&P 500 as an offering in the plan in 2018. A Vanguard spokesperson offered the following explanation: "We believe the Total Stock Market Index Fund is the best proxy for the U.S. market, offering exposure to large-, mid-, and small-cap stocks, whereas Vanguard Institutional Index Fund concentrates on large-cap stocks."

With a Total Market fund, you can go to sleep each night knowing that whatever portion of the U.S. market does well– you will benefit!

MORE IDEAS: Vanguard pioneered index investing, but other well known investment management firms with total market offerings include BlackRock with the iShares Core S&P Total U.S. Stock Market ETF (ITOT), which has 2,500+ holdings; and both Schwab and Fidelity offer Total Market mutual funds: tickers (SWTSX) and (FSKAX) respectively.

Seeking Alpha: ETFs That Have Beaten the S&P 500

Okay– so you've got an aggressive streak in you! You understand that professionals rarely beat the market index. And you understand that most stocks in the S&P 500 don't actually do as well as the S&P. You don't want to pick your own stocks. However, you remain undaunted in a quest to achieve investment returns that exceed the market index. You're a "Shark," and you're not willing to just be average. Should you give up your competitive spirit? Absolutely not!

In fact, there are other index strategies employed by fund management companies that have enjoyed phenomenal returns. And we're not talking about active stock picking. We're just talking about passive index strategies– but different strategies than just owning the S&P 500. Remember the S&P was not created by a higher deity. *Anyone* can create an index, and then build a portfolio of stocks to track it. The S&P 500 is just one species of indexing, other strategies have been more successful.

Here are seven major ETF strategies that have beaten the S&P.

You can use these ETFs to complement your portfolio– not to supplant the S&P. In fact, index funds that track the S&P (like iShare's IVV) or Vanguard's Total U.S. Market (VTI), should make up the lion's share of your domestic equity allocation. But you can consider including one or more of these funds as aggressive growth components. And if they perform as well as they have historically, you can achieve Alpha (returns above the S&P 500) simply by incorporating these funds into your portfolio.

#1 SPDR Dow Jones Industrial Average ETF Trust (DIA)

The SPDR Dow Jones Industrial Average ETF Trust (DIA) managed by State Street is an ETF strategy that long term, has periods of beating the S&P 500. Remember, the S&P 500– as its name suggests– tracks 500 companies. So, one would imagine that among 500 companies, there could be a lot of dogs. In fact we know that the majority of companies that make up the S&P 500 don't do as well as the index!

What's the most quoted Index that you hear on the news? The Dow Jones Industrial Average.

The "Dow," with its 30 stocks, provides investors with a more curated selection of companies. To be a part of the S&P 500, a company needs to have one of the 500 largest market capitalizations. To be a part of the Dow Jones Industrial Average, a company must be considered an indisputable global leader, and among the most important U.S. companies. The DJIA companies are also quite diverse in terms of industry segment.

Current components of the DJIA are: 3M, American Express, Amgen, Apple, Boeing, Caterpillar, Chevron, Cisco, Coca-Cola, DowDuPont, Goldman Sachs, Home Depot, Honeywell, IBM, Intel, Johnson & Johnson, JPMorgan Chase, McDonald's, Merck, Microsoft, Nike, Procter & Gamble, Salesforce, Travelers Companies, United Health, Verizon, Visa, Walmart, Walgreens Boots Alliance, and Walt Disney.

The SPDR DJIA ETF has been outperformed by the S&P over the last five years, but a longer viewpoint tells a different story.

If we go back to the late 1990s, the Dow Jones Industrial Average ETF sports a cumulative return beating the S&P

I'm not going to tout this Dow Jones ETF too much, as the S&P has bested it for 5, 10, and 15 year lookbacks. But we'll include it as a strategy for potentially beating the S&P 500 over multiple decades. It also currently sports a dividend yield of 1.66%, 34 basis points higher than the S&P 500.

#2 Invesco S&P 500 Top 50 (XLG)

Continuing on our theme of a more selective, yet passively managed index, let's take a look at Invesco's S&P 500 Top 50 (XLG).

With this ETF we're selecting the top 50 of the top 500. So, if the S&P represents the 500 biggest market cap companies, Invesco's XLG holds the 50 biggest market cap stocks– the real leviathans– twenty more companies than the previously mentioned Dow Jones fund, and representing the top 10% of the S&P.

If you've watched CNBC or followed other market news lately, you've probably heard Wall Streeters speak of the "Magnificent 7," which are the seven Mega Cap companies. These include: Apple, Microsoft, Google, Amazon, NVIDIA, Meta, and Tesla, which finished out 2023 with a combined market cap of $12.3 trillion. Collectively they rose 75.7% in value in 2023, accounting for a sizeable portion of the gains in the S&P 500, with the rest of the index trading relatively flat. These seven stocks account for nearly 30% of the S&P's total valuation!

What I'm driving at here is that investors might do better than the overall S&P 500 index by just focusing on the top 50 winners.

Over the last year the top 50 stocks are up more than 27% versus the overall 500's 24.5%. Over five years the S&P 500 sported a total return of about 101%, bested by the XLG Top 50's return of 132%.

MORE IDEAS: iShares manages an S&P Top 100 companies (symbol OEF) of the S&P 500 that has also outperformed the larger 500 index. Its 5-year annualized return sits at 16.96% vs. the 500's 15.01%.

#3 Invesco QQQ Trust (QQQ)

I'll have to admit one of my favorite funds, and a position I consider a no-brainer for most equity portfolios, is Invesco's QQQ (often referred to as the Qs). It's often the second biggest equity position in my clients' accounts.

It follows a simple strategy– it owns the 100 largest (based on market capitalization) domestic and international non-financial companies listed on the Nasdaq.

By investing in only Nasdaq listed firms, the index becomes immediately more tech and life sciences focused, but not exclusively so. The big tech names that have rewarded investors over the last 10-15 years– NVIDIA, Apple, Microsoft, Tesla, Google (Alphabet), Amazon, Meta– are all included. But consumer names such as Comcast, Pepsi, Costco, and Starbucks are also among the 25 top names.

Some of the biggest life sciences names are included such as Amgen, Vertex, and Gilead. But the Qs exclusion of financial companies shielded it from the wreckage of Silicon Valley Bank, which traded on the Nasdaq.

The Qs performance is nothing short of spectacular. The fund was up 55% in 2023 versus the Nasdaq Composite's return of 45%.

Over the last 5 years the Qs have delivered a 21.52% annualized return vs. S&P's 15.01% return. Over the last 10 years the Qs annualized return sits at 18.67% vs. the S&P's 12.82%. The Qs 15-year annualized return clocks in at around 19%

If a hedge fund manager could deliver returns like the Qs, he or she would have so much money thrown at them their head would start spinning.

But you don't need to hire a hot-shot hedge fund manager to participate in one of the top wealth creating investment vehicles of the last 15 years. Anyone can invest in the Qs, and all it takes is around $400.00 to buy your first share!

MORE IDEAS: If you like the idea of buying a Nasdaq focused ETF but 100 companies seems too narrow, take a look at Fidelity's ONEQ ETF. This ETF tracks the aforementioned Nasdaq Composite Index (and includes the 1,000 largest Nasdaq companies by market cap). It has also posted S&P beating annualized returns of 18.48% over 5-years, and 16.16% over 10-years.

#4 iShares PHLX Semiconductor ETF (SOXX)

A very undiversified ETF, but tracking one of the hottest industries, is the iShares PHLX Semiconductor, often just referred to as the SOXX.

This ETF seeks to track the investment results of an index composed of U.S.-listed equities in the semiconductor sector. So, unlike the QQQ ETF, this is a single sector ETF and only has 35 holdings.

ETF	5 Year Annualized Return	10 Year Annualized Return
IVV S&P 500	15.01%	12.82%
VTI Total Market	14.06%	12.10%
DIA Dow 30	10.15%	11.14%
QQQ Nasdaq 100	21.52%	18.67%
SOXX Semiconductor	31.44%	25.40%
XLG S&P Top 50	18.30%	14.83%
Technology Select SPDR	24.85%	20.98%
IHI Medical Device	7.33%	13.22%
IWY Russell Top 200	21.04%	17.55%
Performance as of 6/30/2024		

All of the biggest names in the Semiconductor industry are held in this ETF: NVIDIA, Taiwan Semiconductor, Intel, Broadcom, Texas Instruments and 30 others.

Semiconductor chips are powering nearly everything these days. The typical automobile has between 1,000 and 3,000 chips. There is a reason Congress passed the CHIPS Act in 2022, awarding billions to semiconductor manufacturers. As one CNBC commentator recently put it: "semiconductor chips are the new oil."

Any Top-Down macro-view would have to foresee the world having more semiconductors in use 10, 20, 30 years out. The aforementioned Qs have an impressive 5-year annualized return of 21.52%, but that looks pale next to the SOXX's 5-year annualized return of 31.44%. Over 10 years the SOXX has delivered an annualized return of 25.40% vs. the S&P 500's 12.82%.

MORE IDEAS: VanEck Semiconductor ETF (SMH) has racked up similarly impressive results with a 5-year annualized return of 37.67% and 10-year of 28.03%. The fund is more narrowly invested carrying only 25 names. Both SOXX and SMH have annual management expenses of .35% (or 35 basis points).

#5 State Street's Technology Select Sector SPDR ETF (XLK)

We've already identified big tech as an industry that has propelled markets higher over the last couple of decades. State Street's Technology Select Sector SPDR ETF (XLK) seeks to track the investment results of an index composed of equities representing the technology sector of the S&P 500 Index.

The ETF has approximately 70 positions, and top holdings include: NVIDIA, Microsoft, Apple, Broadcom, Salesforce, and Adobe; thus, a strong outlay to Semiconductors (the "new oil") and Software.

Technologist and Venture Capitalist extraordinaire, Marc Andreessen, proclaimed in 2011: "Software is eating the world." Will anyone argue that software is unlikely to play a larger role in various facets of our lives including both work and pleasure? Probably not.

Over the last five years XLK shares have recorded annualized returns of 24.85% vs. S&P's 15.01% return. Over the last 10 years XLK has posted annualized returns of 20.98% vs. the S&P's 12.82%.

MORE IDEAS: Technology specialized ETFs (similar to XLK) that have performed well vs. the S&P 500 the last five years include: iShares U.S. Technology ETF (IYW), Fidelity MSCI Information Technology Index ETF (FTEC), Vanguard Information Technology ETF (VGT), and iShares Global Tech ETF (IXN).

#6 iShares U.S. Medical Devices ETF (IHI)

Another strong sector over the last 10 years has been medical devices, and the iShares U.S. Medical Devices ETF seeks to track the investment results of an index composed of U.S. equities in this sector.

Like the semiconductor index ETF, IHI tracks a narrow index of 55 positions– the leading publicly traded companies in medical devices. Top holdings include: Abbott Laboratories, Medtronic, Stryker, and Boston Scientific.

Returns were absolutely stellar into 2021, but unlike big tech, the last three years have not been kind to healthcare, medical, and biotech stocks.

Even with the subpar recent performance, the fund's long-term gains are aglow with a 13.22% average annualized return over the last 10 years. This compares to the S&P's 12.82% over the same period.

#7 iShares Russell Top 200 Growth (IWY)

Another interesting strategy from BlackRock is their iShares Russell Top 200 Growth ETF (IWY).

Like some of the other ETFs we've discussed, IWY is a bit sleeker carrying only a little over 100 names. As we've emphasized, earnings growth is key to stock market success, and IWY applies filters to the largest U.S. companies by market cap, and then includes companies that exhibit particular growth characteristics. IWY winnows the initial Russell 200 Large Cap names down to the 100 (and change) displaying the top relative growth attributes.

A fund like this differs from the Qs in that it will include New York Stock Exchange (NYSE) companies as well as Nasdaq. As an example, at the time of this writing Eli Lilly, an NYSE company, is the fund's 9th

---

largest holding. Other non-tech, non-Nasdaq companies that make the top 20 cut include: UnitedHealth (UNH), Home Depot (HD), Visa (V), and MasterCard (MA).

And the results have been stunning. The 5-year annualized return sits at 21.04% vs. 15.01% for the S&P 500, and the 10-year annualized return is 17.55% vs. 12.82%.

MORE IDEAS: ETFs with similar strategies of applying growth filters to a basic passive index include: Motley Fool 100 Index ETF (TMFC), Schwab U.S. Large-Cap Growth (SCHG), and Vanguard Mega Cap Growth ETF (MGK). For folks interested in this strategy who value socially responsible investing, the Nuveen ESG Large-Cap Growth ETF (NULG) has been a top performer. Investors can achieve alpha and know that the fund has screened for ESG, controversial business involvement, and low-carbon criteria. NULG has sported annualized returns of 19.18% over the last five years, and 18.94% since its inception in 2016.

Should I Try and Time the Market?

Or better put, should I sell when I *think* the market is high, and should I buy when I *think* the market is low?

Just like trying to get rich quickly is a strong instinct, timing the market seems irresistible to investors– including professionals!

According to innumerable studies, most investors are terrible at predicting short-term swings in the market. More often than not, investors find themselves buying high and selling low.

This makes perfect sense– when the market is experiencing a depressed period– we are depressed. And for maybe good reason. The 2008 Financial Crisis was scary! After all, the Fed Chair and Treasury Secretary were pleading with Congress for a multi-hundred billion dollar bailout of our Financial Institutions. COVID was scary. We were told to stay in our homes, stop going to work, stop shopping unless it's necessary, stop socializing, stop traveling. With events like this, investors are tempted to sell, and then stay out of the market until conditions improve. If you can get out before the s**t hits the fan that can be good, but investors rarely get back into the market in time to enjoy the recovery.

Unfortunately, some of the biggest one-day upswings in the market occur during these volatile periods.

According to *Business Insider*, if an investor stayed fully invested in the S&P 500 from 1983 through 2013, they would've enjoyed an 8.4% annualized return.

However, if trading in and out resulted in missing just the ten best days during that same period, then those annualized returns would collapse to 5.8%.

CNBC cited a longer-term Bank of America study that quantified just how bad it can be for investors who miss out on the market's best days.

Looking at data going back to 1930, BofA found that if an investor held steady through the ups and downs of the Depression, WWII, the '87 crash, the 2008 Financial Crisis– and all of the other innumerable hiccups and Bear markets of the last nine decades– the total return would have been 17,715%.

Remember the data from NYU that I cited earlier in the book? That 17,715% return represents all the phenomenal growth from the Great Depression era to modern times. And if an investor wasn't in the market for the 10 best days per decade, the total return plummets to 28%. You read that right– instead of getting a 17,000+ percentage return, you get 28%.

LESSON LEARNED: Don't get out of the market! Be patient, stay in the market, and don't miss the best trading days.

According to a study cited by investment manager Dimensional (which manages the well-known DFA funds), markets often bounce back quickly. On average, just one year after a market decline of 10%, stocks have rebounded 12.5%. After a decline of 20%, the three-year cumulative return tops 40%.

In fact, equity returns are often strongest after a decline. The average cumulative 5-year return, immediately following a 20% decline, is 72%.

Just look at 2023, when the market cratered in late October as the yield on the 10-year Treasury touched 5%. If you got out of the market in late October– or were already out of the market and didn't get back in– you missed out on a phenomenal recovery. In less than 2 months, the S&P went from 4,100 to nearly 4,800, a 17% bounce off the lows.

Dollar Cost Averaging

If I don't time the market, what should I do? Dollar Cost Average!!!!

Dollar Cost Averaging is a very simple strategy that allows investors to accumulate positions in equities at various price points. Let's say you arrange to have $100.00 withdrawn from your bank account on the 15th of each month and invested in the S&P 500. The S&P will change month to month, but your $100.00 contribution remains the same.

If in month one the index fund costs $100.00, you'll pick up 1 share. If in month two there is a horrible bear market and the index fund plum-

HOW DOLLAR COST AVERAGING WORKS

Invest **equal** amounts at **regular** intervals

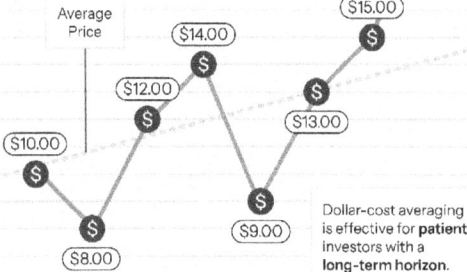

$20.00

Zero Stress

Average Price

$15.00

$14.00

$12.00

$13.00

$10.00

Dollar-cost averaging is effective for **patient** investors with a **long-term horizon**.

$9.00

$8.00

The key to dollar-cost averaging is to always **buy at a regular interval** regardless of whether the market is up or down. An **index fund** is the perfect vehicle.

mets to $50.00, you'll pick up 2 shares. If in month three the market recovers to $100.00, you'll pick up 1 share. In three months you've invested a total of $300.00, and you bought four shares. The market lost half its value and then recovered. But because you also bought when the market was down (in month two), those shares doubled in value. So after three months, you own four shares of a $100.00 fund. Your $300.00 invested has grown to $400.00 (a 33% gain) even though the market didn't go up. It only recovered to its initial position.

Investors utilizing corporate 401(k)s and organizational 403(b)s are naturally employing Dollar Cost Averaging. You get paid regularly, and funds are going directly out of your paycheck and into the market. You are buying weekly, semi-monthly, monthly– or whatever your pay interval. If the market is up, and you get paid– you buy. If the market is down, and you get paid– you buy. All of these different price points average out.

This is why 401(k)s offer such a tremendous opportunity for investors to develop wealth. Without even thinking about it, they are employing three important principles shared in this book:

1) They are often indexing– Online financial site *Plansponsor* cited a 2019 study conducted by Brightscope/ICI which revealed retirement plan participants are investing 33% of their assets in index funds, double the figure from 2006. As we discussed, an index fund is usually far superior to actively managed funds in performance, and offers lower fees.

2) They are being patient– Since investors can't touch their retirement funds (without incurring a penalty) until they are 59 ½, it forces them to leave their funds in the market for longer periods of time.

3) They are Dollar Cost Averaging– As described, the fact that investors typically have funds automatically withdrawn from their paychecks and invested without the investor making decisions about whether the market is too high or too low, means the investor will buy at an average of the year's high and low price points.

How to Get Rich Without Really Trying!

Everyone wants to be a millionaire, right? Well here's a simple way to get there– SLOWLY!

Albert Einstein reportedly referred to compound interest as the eighth wonder of the world. He went on to state that those who understand it, earn it and those who don't, will pay it. Let's understand it and make it work for us.

Let's utilize our Dollar Cost Averaging strategy and see how the magic of compound interest will grow our money.

Let's imagine we are 35 years old, and we've hopefully saved a little money and have the capacity to save a bit more each month. We'll start with $10,000 and invest it today in the S&P 500. If the S&P grows 10% (its historic return figure), by the end of the year we'll have $11,000. And if the S&P grows 10% again in year two, our $11,000 will grow to $12,100. We've earned a return on top of our return. So, imagine a continuous growth trajectory over 30 years.

And let's imagine we have the capacity to add to this kitty each month, and we'll save an additional $420.00 a month for the next 30 years.

If we employ this strategy, how much money will we have? Drum roll please.......................$1,000,000!!! Or, $1,003,543.90 to be exact. We did it– now we're a millionaire! Forget about needing to winning the lottery.

And all we did was engage in a disciplined strategy and let the magic of compounding returns grow our wealth. While Warren Buffett may be an investing genius, he attributes his success to the same science of compounding returns: "My wealth has come from a combination of living in America, some lucky genes, and compound interest."

This is a very simple strategy to employ and many people are already utilizing similar strategies in their retirement funds.

Do I Need to Invest in International Stocks?

It's not a bad idea, but it's not necessary. Be careful making international stock investments. It's easy to be steered by the commonplace ads displaying how the U.S. market has rarely been the best performing market over some 20-year period. These ads are often issued by mutual fund companies seeking to promote their international offerings.

The ad will typically show a trailing 10-year graph that displays the performance of the S&P 500 juxtaposed with the best performing international equity market of a given year. For instance, in 2019 the best performing market worldwide was Greece with a 50.20% return. The S&P was pretty strong, but only posted a 30.67% return. Let's take a look at 2017 when Argentina led the world with a 53.87% return, more than doubling the S&P 500's seemingly paltry 21.21%. And we could continue across the decades: there is always a foreign market somewhere that outpaces the U.S. These charts can lure investors into thinking that the U.S. market is for old boring fuddy-duddies, and that the real action is abroad.

In a study of international and U.S. equity performance from 1950-2016, the U.S. portfolio sported annualized returns of 11.2%. The international portfolio trailed the U.S. by 190 basis points with a 9.3% return. The study showed that a globally balanced portfolio of 70/30 U.S. and foreign stocks would generate a standard deviation (which measures volatility) of 13.2%, whereas the standard deviation for U.S.-only was 14.3%. Because there is occasional inverse correlation between U.S. and foreign markets, a balanced portfolio during the time period studied offered a smoother, less volatile ride.

While we can't argue with the historical data, we can certainly claim that 1950 to 2016 was a period that saw fast growing economies in Europe and Japan. In fact, the Japanese stock market (Nikkei) roared for decades reaching a colossal peak price of nearly 39,000 in 1989. It took two decades for the Japanese stock market to crater at around 5,600 in 2009. As we'll discuss in a minute, Japan has lost its stature as a fast-growing economy.

U.S. vs. International Stocks	5 year	10 year
Vanguard S&P 500 (VOO)	15.01%	12.82%
Vanguard Total International (VXUS)	5.80%	4.05%
Vanguard Emerging Markets (VWO)	3.71%	3.02%
Vanguard Devloped Markets (VEA)	6.60%	4.54%
Fund Performance as of 6/30/2024	Source: Vanguard	

Vanguard's VXUS is a great ETF for providing international exposure. It invests in 8,500 international stocks; essentially owning the entire international market (outside the U.S.)– both developed and emerging countries.

However, look at the returns of VXUS relative to the S&P. If you were in this fund directly, or via a Vanguard target fund (which utilizes VXUS) often with 30% of total assets allocated to international exposure, you'd be very disappointed– for not just 5 but 10 years!

Can international diversification be "di-worse-ification"? Be careful with what percentage of your equity assets are in international funds. While international exposure may provide inverse correlation to U.S. markets, when the results are staggeringly poor, what's so great about inverse correlation?

The inverse correlation– meaning foreign markets doing well when the U.S. market does poorly– has existed primarily in emerging markets, not developed markets. Over the last 15 years, developed markets are relatively "coupled" with U.S. markets, doing either the same or slightly worse. Whereas emerging markets have had periods of significant out-performance vs. U.S. markets.

For my clients, I typically recommend initially allocating only 10% of their equity assets to international focused ETFs. Compare my recommended 10% allocation with the typical 30% (of total assets) in a Target Fund (frequently used in employer retirement plans).

Let's be honest– the U.S. offers the safest and most dynamic financial markets.

Do you remember in the mid-2000s when talk of BRIC (Brazil, Russia, India, and China) stocks was all the rage?

I owned some Russian stocks and ETFs that performed well for awhile. Guess where they went after Russia invaded Ukraine? My shares in Yandex, often known as the Google of Russia, became inaccessible as trading in the stock was suspended.

And with the saber-rattling China has engaged in over Taiwan, how safe are Chinese investments?

Brazil has see-sawed back and forth between leftist and ultra-right governments.

Of the BRIC countries, only India has remained a predictable and profitable opportunity (for now).

And how about developed markets, which include Western Europe, Canada, Australia, Japan, and South Korea? Both Japan and South Korea suffer from astonishingly low birth rates, which ultimately threaten their economies.

Western Europe also suffers from lower birth rates and very mature markets. Countries like Italy (with high pension contribution costs) and

Switzerland (where the minimum capital requirement to start a business is $120,000) simply don't embrace dynamic entrepreneurship and easy capital formation like the U.S. America continues to attract many of the best and brightest individuals from around the world who wish to pursue their entrepreneurial dreams.

I'm not a xenophobe or U.S.-centric isolationist by any stretch of the imagination. I love traveling the world and have friends from every continent (excluding Antarctica of course). However, when it comes to my stock market investments, I'm sticking with the "Good Ol' U.S. of A" for 90% of my equity allocation. I certainly hope that my 10% international allocation does well. And I won't rebalance it each year. So, if it becomes 15% of my equity holdings– that's fine. I hope future decades bring peace and economic prosperity for all. But if I need equity growth to put my children through college and fund my retirement, I think the U.S. offers the most predictable opportunity.

My point is buttressed by the fact that the U.S. stock market has had the second best average annualized return over the last 10 years. While countries like Argentina, Denmark, and Taiwan have had better 5-year returns, the U.S. has led 40+ different global markets (excluding Argentina) with an annualized 10-year return exceeding 12%.

PART X

FINAL THOUGHTS

INVESTING IS HARD! If the professionals can't beat the market, we should assume that it's difficult for amateurs to beat the market as well. We've discussed strategies that the individual investor can utilize to do better than the index, but we should never assume that there is any guarantee we'll be successful.

And we should also never assume that the market will perform exactly as it has in the past.

Yes– over 90 years, the market has delivered a wonderful annualized return of nearly 10%, but there is no guarantee that the next 10 years or 90 years will deliver comparable returns.

This may sound perplexing, but most stocks within the S&P 500 do not beat the market average. According to S&P Dow Jones Indices, only 22% of the stocks in the S&P 500 outperformed the index itself from 2000 to 2020. That means if you are picking individual stocks yourself, many of the companies you choose will likely not do as well as the index.

Over the measurement period (2000 to 2020), the S&P 500 gained 322%, while the median stock rose by just 63%.

THE SHARK INVESTOR
FINAL THOUGHTS

How can this be? According to Craig Lazara of Dow Jones Indices, it is because there are often just a handful of stocks that have exceptional performance, and generate an outsized portion of the S&P 500's return.

"Rather than being symmetrically distributed around an average, return distributions typically have a very long right tail; a relatively small number of excellent performers has a disproportionate influence on the market's overall return."

Here's an even more depressing metric to consider– while the stock market has generally gone up, most individual stocks either go down, or disappear.

According to an article written by John Rekenthaler, Morningstar's Director of Research, most U.S. stocks are not worth owning. Rekenthaler simulated work conducted by Hendrik Bessembinder, a finance professor at the W.P. Carey School of Business at Arizona State University. Looking at the results of the 5,000 largest publicly traded U.S. equities beginning in January 2011 and

"He lost his head over an investment."

concluding in December 2020, Rekenthaler found that only 42% of the securities finished up, 36% finished down, and 22% were gone. "Although the Morningstar U.S. Stock Index enjoyed a 13.90% annualized gain for the decade, only 42% of individual equities finished in the black. Nearly as many (36%) posted 10-year losses. The final 22% vanished."

While Rekenthaler did not investigate the fates of the vanished stocks, he cited research that suggests half the expired equities were acquired with decent results, while the other half were delisted, due to distressed outcomes.

According to a *Kiplinger* article, also citing the work of Professor Bessembinder, only a small percentage of stocks actually deliver desirable returns: "Not only do the majority of stocks deliver long-term under performance vs. pretty much the least risky asset you can find, but the great bulk of equity-market wealth is created by just a tiny percentage of the very best stocks."

Kiplinger cited Bessembinder's study of the performance of more than 64,000 global stocks from January 1990 to December 2020. His research revealed that the compound returns of 55.2% of U.S. stocks, as well as 57.4% of non-U.S. stocks, underperformed essentially risk-free one-month U.S. Treasury bills.

An even scarier revelation was that the entirety of the $75.7 trillion in net global stock market wealth created over the past 30 years was generated solely by the top-performing 2.4% of stocks!

More BAD News: You Are Not Guaranteed to Make Money Owning an Index Fund!

Are you guaranteed to make money in stocks if you hold an S&P 500 Index ETF for 5 years or 10 years? Is it a given that you will attain the widely-bandied 10% per year in-line with the historical averages?

Absolutely not.

Unfortunately, you might need to have at least a 15-20 year time horizon to make money. While that may seem like an awfully long time period in order to achieve investment results, let's just take a look at a couple of very bad periods in the market.

In 1966 the Dow Jones Industrial Average peaked at 1,000, and in 1982 the Dow cratered at 769. An investor buying at the peak in 1966 was down 25% 16 years later.

And more recently, investors experienced zero return for most of the 2000s. In 1997 the Dow Jones Industrial Average first crossed 7,000 points and in 2009 the Dow hit a low of 7,000.

That means the market goes through cycles of a decade or more where there may be little upward movement.

Thus, if you have bad timing and end up buying at peaks and selling during downturns, your returns will be particularly disappointing. One can only imagine the frustration of an investor who funds their eight-year old's 529 college savings plan with a significant stock allocation, only to see the investment do nothing for 10 years.

This is why asset allocation is absolutely key for your portfolio. You should have some portion of your investments in securities that are fixed, and provide a predictable rate of return like bonds, CDs, and preferred stocks.

"Stern's Law": Investment Corollary to "Murphy's Law"

Be prepared for frustration! Along with many worthwhile endeavors in life, trying to make money in the stock market can be challenging. We all know Murphy's Law– often abbreviated as "If anything can go wrong, it will." The pursuit of stock market riches isn't exempt from the peculiar ubiquity and gravity of this law. One of the unfortunate and indelible things I've learned about investing over the years is that the market usually behaves in a manner contrary to your wishes. We'll call this "Stern's Law," and it has three irritating components:

1) Whenever you are considering investing in a stock and you are performing your due diligence, the stock will move up. Every day you perform your homework, the stock will continue to move higher. You'll say to yourself, "Oh my God– I've got to get into this thing now!"

2) So, you'll suspend your due diligence, rush through your research, and you'll go ahead and buy shares; and soon after your purchase, the stock will promptly lose 20%.

3) Now you'll sit and watch it everyday piddling in a trading range: a little up, a little down, a little up, a little down, etc. You'll become impatient with the company. It hasn't moved up in months, it seems stagnant, and somehow you've picked a stock that Wall Street doesn't care about. And you'll sell. And

MURPHY'S LAW

Nothing is as easy as it looks. Everything takes longer than you expect. And if anything can go wrong, it will, at the worst possible moment.

STERN'S LAW

Every day you are researching a stock it will increase in price, causing you to be impatient. As soon as you buy the stock, it will go down. It will then likely meander for months, creating additional impatience. As soon as you sell said stock, it will rocket to new highs.

I guarantee you, soon after you sell, the shares will rally to new highs! The company will announce a major earnings beat or that it's getting acquired, and you'll ceaselessly beat yourself up over your impatience.

Even Warren Buffett experienced a taste of "Stern's Law" in one of his earliest stock picks. When the "Oracle of Omaha" was eleven, he picked up three shares of Cities Service Preferred at $38.00 as well as a few shares for his sister. The stock immediately declined to $27.00, and he was incessantly pestered by his sister. It finally recovered to $40.00 whereupon Buffett sold both his own and his sister's shares. Shortly after his sale, Cities Service took off like a rocket ship soaring to $200.00.

How to Counter "Stern's Law"

Fortunately, we have already introduced and suggested new investor behaviors to help fight off these evil "Stern's Law" forces that imperil our investments and make us look foolish. Here's the antidote:

1) Don't worry if XYZ stock goes from $20.00 to $23.00 while you're

doing your research. Remember, we are in this for the long haul. We want to know if XYZ stock is going to $80.00 a share, maybe $200.00 a share. So, continue with your due diligence, and don't worry about a price increase that– in the long term– will be insignificant.

2) If you buy the stock and the share price goes down, maybe it's a good time to buy more? You just did your research, you determined it's a great stock to own, and now it's cheaper. As I discussed earlier, in my personal investing experience when I first bought Baidu (known as the Google of China), it promptly lost 20% of its value. I bought more shares, and now the stock is up 10-fold.

3) Don't get completely impatient. If the stock does nothing for a while, just relax; you are in this for the long term. Re-read the section on "Laggards." And even if you can't resist selling, don't sell *all* your shares! Leave some on the table. So, if the company does get acquired or has a major announcement propelling its shares, you're still in the game!

Efficient Market Hypothesis

The Efficient Market Hypothesis, or EMH, is a financial theory that declares stock prices reflect all publicly available information. It holds that the price of a security is an accurate representation of everything that can be known about a company, and at no time are securities overvalued or undervalued. An extension of EMH is the Efficient Market Theory, which states that it is impossible to beat the market, or consistently produce more than average returns. Moreover, the EMH also suggests that it is impossible for an investor to find undervalued stocks or sell stocks at a premium.

THE SHARK INVESTOR
FINAL THOUGHTS

Burton Malkiel, author of the classic *A Random Walk Down Wall Street*, has been a vocal advocate of the Efficient Market thesis for decades. While my respect for Malkiel is immense, I find it somewhat odd that he begins his great tome on efficient markets by citing centuries of speculative bubbles. In fact, almost the entirety of Part I of *A Random Walk...* is an exposition on the extraordinary pricing bubbles that investors have engaged in from the Dutch tulip bulb mania to the Dot Com debacle.

> **"A market where there are a huge number of rational, profit-maximizers actively competing, with each trying to predict the future market values of individual securities, and where important current information is almost freely available to all participants."**
>
> *-Eugene Fama*

Noted as one of the early important economists contributing to EMH, Eugene Fama wrote that an Efficient Market exists in: "A market where there are a huge number of rational profit-maximizers actually competing, with each trying to predict the future market values of individual securities, and where important current information is almost freely available to participants."

When I read this sentence there appears to be a glaring flaw: the use of the word "rational." If the pool of stock market investors only consisted of institutional investors, then Fama's proclamation of the market being efficient would have more legs.

But the stock market is also influenced by irrational, uneducated investors who treat stock picking in a similar manner to casino gambling.

Many investors who influence prices are not rational. They have limited knowledge of how to value securities, and are instead only captivated by the possibility that they might go up quickly. We witnessed this in the 1960s Go-Go period, the Dot Com bubble, and again with COVID-era Meme stock investing. Uneducated participants get involved in influencing stock valuations and distortions of pricing take place. Malkiel documents these distortions in great detail in *A Random Walk…*

In fact, Malkiel describes how even the industry professionals, not just amateurs, get caught up in irrational behavior. He notes how internet bubble analysts like Mary Meeker and Henry Blodgett potentially touted securities they followed in order to win investment banking business for their respective firms. Blodgett stated traditional valuation metrics didn't matter with the explosion of internet technology. Meeker, in a 1999 portrait, was quoted proclaiming that the late 1990's was an investment era to be "rationally reckless." If the industry professionals declare that traditional valuation metrics don't matter, then in what world do Fama's rational participants exist?

EMH + Conclusion

If EMH is accurate, then investors like Warren Buffett, Peter Lynch, George Soros, and Jim Rogers should not exist. Yet their successful careers appear to dictate that the application of an investment discipline can produce returns that exceed the S&P for long periods of time. The EMH theorist will assign the success of these investors as rare anomalies and the experience of exceedingly good luck, not skill.

But the luck viewpoint also completely dismisses the very success-

THE SHARK INVESTOR
FINAL THOUGHTS

ful "investment" careers of Jeff Bezos, Bill Gates, Mark Zuckerberg, Jensen Huang, Larry Page, Sergey Brin, Larry Ellison, Reed Hastings, Michael Dell, Phillip Knight and dozens of other successful CEOs who made very rational decisions to HOLD the equity in their companies for multiple decades. These founders may have gained their shares through their initial contribution of intellectual capital, but they made continuous rational decisions to HOLD their shares and not radically diversify. Jeff Bezos might have become a billionaire just shortly after Amazon's IPO in 1997. But he became a centi-billionaire by holding onto a substantial number of his shares for 25+ years.

Would an EMH theorist have advised Bezos to sell all of his shares and buy an index fund– insisting there was no way for Bezos to attain above-market returns for multiple decades? Bezos believed he had a "wonderful" business. Investors like Buffett and Lynch love to buy "wonderful" businesses with great managers and hold them for extended periods.

Bezos remained bullish on Amazon for 25 years, and any individual investor could have attained the same multi-decade, 30% annualized returns that Bezos captured.

Yes– it will require luck to be successful, as no one can foretell the future. Will a company continue to grow earnings at 25% for the next 20 years? No analysis, whether Top Down, Technical, or Fundamental can provide the answer.

Remember, Mark Zuckerberg thought he was creating a Harvard-only dating site when he founded Facebook. Sergey Brin and Larry Page thought they were starting a search engine that might be used in academia when they founded Google. Jeff Bezos thought he was starting a bookstore when he founded Amazon.

Even the entrepreneurs can't foresee their journeys. So, absolutely– the EMH theorists are partially right– luck is an ingredient. But luck should not be discounted as purely magical. Perfectly applicable here is the wise saying that "luck exists when opportunity meets preparation." Or put another way, it often takes a lot of skill to be lucky.

This book has given you the tools to be prepared. You have learned how to be a "Shark Investor." You will be highly discerning and patient. You will invest only in companies that you understand with highly scalable, efficient business models. You will avoid "Nosebleed Valuations." And you will pounce when you sense the opportunity to buy stock in the company of a visionary CEO, who will disrupt and reward shareholders with years of above average earnings growth.

As Yoda teaches the Jedi: "Patience you must have young Padawan."

You are prepared. Now I wish you luck.

THE SHARK INVESTOR

NOTES:

What's So Great About the Stock Market?
1. https://www.biggerpockets.com/renewsblog/real-estate-vs-stocks-performance/
2. http://pages.stern.nyu.edu/~adamodar/New_Home_Page/datafile/histretSP.html
3. https://www.fool.com/investing/general/2016/04/22/how-have-stocks-fared-the-last-50-years-youll-be-s.aspx
4. https://www.forbes.com/advisor/investing/stock-and-bond-returns/
5. https://www.bedelfinancial.com/what-investment-could-beat-owning-an-nfl-team
6. https://www.statista.com/statistics/193435/average-franchise-value-in-the-nfl-since-2000/
7. https://arttactic.com/editorial/quick-profits-on-art-investments-forget-it/
8. https://www.investopedia.com/ask/answers/020915/has-gold-been-good-investment-over-long-term.asp
9. Jeremy Siegel, *Stocks for the Long Run*, McGraw Hill, 2014

What is This Thing Called the S&P 500?
1. https://www.marketwatch.com/tools/mutual-fund/top25largest

What Percentage of Fund Managers Outperform the S&P 500?
1. http://fortune.com/2017/04/13/stock-indexes-beat-mutual-funds/
2. https://www.cnbc.com/2017/02/27/active-fund-managers-rarely-beat-their-benchmarks-year-after-year.html
3. https://www.kiplinger.com/article/investing/t052-c023-s002-why-we-re-better-buyers-than-sellers.html

Can I Really Get A Leg Up On Wall Street?
1. https://topforeignstocks.com/2017/10/01/average-stock-holding-period-on-nyse-1929-to-2016/
2. https://www.forbes.com/sites/simonmoore/2019/11/16/how-you-can-make-money-copying-hedge-funds/

Beat the Street by Not Being "Trigger Happy"
1. https://www.learnstockmarket.in/quote/nobody-wants-to-get-rich-slowly-

warren-buffett/
2. https://icfs.com/financial-knowledge-center/turnover-ratios-and-how-compute-them
3. https://www.investopedia.com/articles/mutualfund/09/mutual-fund-turnover-rate.asp

...And You Don't Have to Buy Hot Tech Stocks!
1. https://www.nasdaq.com/articles/this-monster-stock-is-the-best-performer-of-the-last-25-years
2. https://www.cnbc.com/2024/02/17/monster-energy-drink-stock-is-best-performer-of-the-last-30-years.html
3. https://stockanalysis.com/markets/gainers/5y/

How Do Venture Capitalists Get Rich?
1. https://visible.vc/blog/startup-funding-stages/

Stay In Your Lane...
1. https://money.cnn.com/interactive/economy/my-american-success-story-daymond-john/index.html
2. https://lorigreiner.com/

Don't Obsess Over Current Valuation Like "Mr. Wonderful"
1. https://www.investopedia.com/news/biggest-winners-uber-ipo/
2. https://www.forbes.com/sites/lensherman/2023/01/16/ubers-new-math-increase-prices-and-squeeze-driver-pay/

Barbara Corcoran: People Person
1. https://www.cnbc.com/2023/07/03/barbara-corcoran-on-the-shark-tank-deal-that-made-her-468-million.html
2. https://www.cnbc.com/2020/03/16/shark-tank-barbara-corcoran-invested-in-a-company-with-no-sales.html

Mark Cuban: The Visionary
1. https://www.forbes.com/profile/mark-cuban/
2. https://www.nasdaq.com/articles/mark-cubans-4-most-lucrative-shark-tank-investments
3. https://www.sportskeeda.com/pop-culture/beatbox-beverages-up-

date-what-happened-mark-cuban-invested-business-shark-tank

4. https://beatboxbeverages.com/blogs/highlights/beatbox-beverages-will-return-to-abc-on-february-4th-for-a-shark-tank-follow-up-with-mark-cuban-on-beyond-the-tank

Robert Herjavec: People Person II

1. https://www.cnbc.com/2019/02/22/robert-herjavecs-liberal-arts-degree-taught-him-this-important-business-skill.html
2. Gail DeGeorge, *The Making of a Blockbuster*, Wiley, 1997

Chris Sacca: Spread Your Bets

1. https://markets.businessinsider.com/news/stocks/billionaire-investor-chris-sacca-startup-investing-venture-capital-tips-amateurs-2021-3-1030219088

SUMMARY: The Shark Thesis

1. https://finance.yahoo.com/news/trade-desk-ttd-risen-136-163332369.html

What Makes Stocks Go Up?

1. https://www.nasdaq.com/market-activity/stocks/nvda/historical
2. https://www.globenewswire.com/news-release/2010/02/17/1149827/0/en/NVIDIA-Reports-Financial-Results-for-Fourth-Quarter-and-Fiscal-Year-2010.html
3. https://www.cnbc.com/2024/01/18/mark-zuckerberg-indicates-meta-is-spending-billions-on-nvidia-ai-chips.html
4. https://www.fool.com/investing/2022/12/30/just-how-badly-did-stock-markets-perform-in-2022/
5. https://www.wsj.com/economy/central-banking/fed-holds-rates-steady-and-sees-cuts-next-year-4d554e9f

Understanding Market Capitalization

1. https://financialengines.com/education-center/small-large-mid-caps-market-capitalization/

Fundamental Analysis vs. Top-Down Analysis

1. John Train, *The New Money Masters*, HarperPerennial, 1989
2. Jim Rogers, *Hot Commodities*, Random House, 2007

3. https://www.nytimes.com/2008/01/13/realestate/13deal2.html
4. https://www.quantifiedstrategies.com/jim-rogers/

Value Investing vs. Growth Investing
1. https://business.columbia.edu/heilbrunn/about/valueinvestinghistory

Always Buy Growth, And It's Not Bad if You Can Get Value as Well!
1. https://www.yardeni.com/pub/sp500revearngr.pdf

Peter Lynch
1. Peter Lynch, *One Up On Wall Street*, Simon and Schuster, 1989
2. Peter Lynch, *Beating the Street*, Simon and Schuster, 1993
3. https://www.networkworld.com/article/2229885/cisco-s-storied-past-as-the-most-valuable-company-on-earth.html
4. https://www.kiplinger.com/investing/how-stock-spinoffs-work
5. *Boston Business Journal*, January 5-11, 2024 Vol. 43, No.47
6. https://www.aar.org/wp-content/uploads/2020/07/AAR-Chronology-Americas-Freight-Railroads-Fact-Sheet.pdf
7. https://www.jstor.org/stable/3694731
8. https://en.wikipedia.org/wiki/Genzyme
9. https://www.investopedia.com/articles/stocks/08/buffett-best-buys.asp
10. https://time.com/2837247/most-profitableproducts/

The Downside of Peter Lynch's Magellan
1. https://seekingalpha.com/article/4157192-keys-to-financial-success-how-behavioral-tendencies-can-impact-accumulation-and-transition
2. https://www.forbes.com/sites/forbesfinancecouncil/2021/06/02/how-investors-are-costing-themselves-money/

Warren Buffett
1. Roger Loewenstein, *Making of an American Capitalist*, Random House, 1995
2. John Train, *The Midas Touch*, HarperCollins, 1995
3. Bob Ivy, "Wannabe Warren," *Forbes*, July 2024, p. 56
4. https://fortune.com/company/berkshire-hathaway/
5. https://pictureperfectportfolios.com/warren-buffetts-views-on-economic-moats-analysis/

6. https://markets.businessinsider.com/news/stocks/warren-buffett-berk-shire-hathaway-asset-bubble-speculation-leverage-financial-crisis-2022-1
7. https://www.bloomberg.com/news/articles/2011-08-15/pfiz-er-wins-viagra-patent-infringement-case-against-teva-pharmaceuticals
8. https://www.berkshirehathaway.com/letters/2007ltr.pdf
9. https://money.com/value-investing-embraces-tech/
10. Andrew Kilpatrick, *Warren Buffett: The Good Guy of Wall Street*, Donald I. Fine, 1992
11. https://www.goodreads.com/work/quotes/25195056-berkshire-hatha-way-letters-to-shareholders
12. https://www.gurufocus.com/news/1974484/warren-buffetts-punch-card-approach
13. https://www.linkedin.com/pulse/what-would-warren-buffett-make-stock-market-silly-season-tom-bradley/
14. https://www.cnbc.com/2018/09/14/warren-buffetts-rule-for-investing-during-the-financial-crisis.html

Herbert Wertheim: The Billionaire You've Never Heard Of
1. https://www.forbes.com/sites/maddieberg/2019/02/19/the-greatest-inves-tor-youve-never-heard-of-an-optometrist-who-beat-the-odds-to-become-a-billionaire/

Another Patient Billionaire
1. https://markets.businessinsider.com/news/stocks/warren-buf-fett-forbes-400-stewart-horejsi-berkshire-hathaway-wealth-billion-aires-2023-10
2. https://www.bloomberg.com/news/articles/2013-09-19/berkshire-shares-turned-a-buy-and-hold-buffett-fan-into-a-billionaire
3. https://ridgewoodinvestments.com/billionaire-from-just-one-great-idea
4. https://nairametrics.com/2021/07/05/how-stewart-horejsi-became-a-bil-lionaire-from-one-investment/

What's a Good P/E?
1. https://www.valuescopeinc.com/resources/white-papers/the-sp-500-pe-ra-tio-a-historical-perspective/

Profit Margin: How Easily Are Profits Created

1. https://www.barrons.com/articles/buy-most-profitable-companies-stocks-simple-strategy-right-margins-return-on-equity-51602529870
2. https://pages.stern.nyu.edu/~adamodar/New_Home_Page/datafile/margin.html

Price to Sales Ratio
1. https://finance.yahoo.com/news/15-most-profitable-industries-america-164322537.html
2. https://www.macrotrends.net/stocks/charts/SNOW/snowflake/price-sales
3. https://www.gurufocus.com/economic_indicators/4238/sp-500-price-to-sales
4. https://www.investors.com/etfs-and-funds/sectors/sp500-warren-buffett-crushes-elon-musk-on-an-increasingly-key-measure/

Buy Companies You Do Business With, or See Others Using the Product
1. https://www.referenceforbusiness.com/history2/11/Waterhouse-Investor-Services-Inc.html
2. https://www.technologyreview.com/2016/07/25/158663/what-yahoo-got-right/

Know Your CEO
1. https://www.morningbrew.com/daily/stories/2019/04/24/masayoshi-son-s-human

Buy Stocks with Founder/ CEOs
1. https://www.forbes.com/profile/niraj-shah/
2. https://www.bizjournals.com/boston/news/2023/03/20/wayfair-spending-on-ceo-personal-security.html
3. https://www.inc.com/stephanie-mehta/founders-are-among-the-most-fairly-paid-ceos-on-the-russell-3000.html
4. https://aflcio.org/paywatch/highest-paid-ceos

Buy a "Toll Road"
1. https://www.gurufocus.com/news/1034046/the-tollbridge-business-products-with-few-substitutes
2. https://www.forbes.com/sites/joannmuller/2012/01/12/why-one-rich-man-shouldnt-own-an-international-bridge/

3. https://www.wilx.com/2024/01/04/new-bridge-connecting-detroit-canada-wont-open-until-fall-2025/
4. https://www.thenationalnews.com/business/technology/2024/01/31/google-alphabet-earnings/
5. https://www.cnbc.com/2023/01/10/apple-app-store-revenue-update-shows-slowing-growth-.html
6. https://www.forrester.com/blogs/apple-sales-and-profits-analysis-for-fy-2023-top-10-insights/

Contemplate the Evolution of the Company
1. https://www.kleinerperkins.com/case-study/amazon/

Buy Disruptors
1. https://www.cnbc.com/2018/05/22/meet-the-2018-cnbc-disruptor-50-companies.html
2. https://www.cnbc.com/quotes/.dsrpt

Buy Companies With Economic Moats
1. https://finance.yahoo.com/news/warren-buffett-explains-moat-principle-164442359.html

Engage in a Controlled "Spray and Pray"
1. https://www.indexologyblog.com/2021/05/12/equity-diversity-and-inclusion/
2. https://www.nber.org/be/20222/how-do-startup-founders-fare-venture-capitalists
3. https://www.fastcompany.com/3003827/why-most-venture-backed-companies-fail

Forget About Technical Analysis
1. https://www.fool.com/investing/value/2009/02/27/avoid-the-mistake-that-cost-buffett-8-years-of-bet.aspx
2. https://www.forbes.com/sites/rickferri/2014/06/02/technical-analysis-drags-down-performance

Be Wary of "Fake" Technology Companies
1. https://vocal.media/geeks/how-much-do-taxi-business-owners-make-

THE SHARK INVESTOR

in-2023
2. https://en.wikipedia.org/wiki/WeWork
3. https://stockanalysis.com/stocks/wewkq/revenue/
4. https://www.nbcnews.com/business/business-news/wework-imploded-2019-pandemic-brought-it-back-life-n1267957
5. https://stockanalysis.com/stocks/wewkq/revenue/
6. https://www.nbcnews.com/business/business-news/wework-imploded-2019-pandemic-brought-it-back-life-n1267957
7. https://hbr.org/2019/08/no-wework-isnt-a-tech-company-heres-why-that-matters

Forget About "Meme" Stocks
1. https://www.fool.com/research/poll-how-well-did-meme-stock-investors-understand/
2. Ben Mezrich, *The Antisocial Network*, Grand Central Publishing, 2021
3. https://www.cnet.com/personal-finance/investing/stock-market/gamestop-what-happened-after-everyday-stock-traders-rocked-wall-street/

Forget About Margin
1. https://www.fool.com/investing/2022/09/29/warren-buffett-doesnt-borrow-money-to-buy-stocks-a/

Forget About Market Gurus
1. https://www.wealthmanagement.com/equities/inaccuracy-market-forecasts

Forget About Options
1. https://www.investopedia.com/trading/options-strategies/
2. https://mitsloan.mit.edu/ideas-made-to-matter/retail-investors-lose-big-op-tions-markets-research-shows
3. https://news.warrington.ufl.edu/faculty-and-research/retail-investors-play-a-losing-game-with-complex-options-according-to-research/
4. John Train, *The New Money Masters*, HarperPerennial, 1989

Forget About Active Investing
1. https://tradeciety.com/24-statistics-why-most-traders-lose-money

Forget About Short Selling

1. https://faculty.wharton.upenn.edu/wp-content/uploads/2012/04/Holding-on---Version-42.pdf

Be Willing to Buy Unprofitable Companies
1. https://www.fool.com/investing/2019/02/09/how-are-sp-500-stocks-chosen.aspx
2. https://www.cnbc.com/2015/03/02/cnbc-excerpts-billionaire-investor-warren-buffett-on-cnbcs-squawk-box-today.html
3. https://investors.palantir.com/news-details/2024/Palantir-Reports-Revenue-Growth-of-21-Year-Over-Year-and-Sixth-Consecutive-Quarter-of-GAAP-Profitability-GAAP-EPS-of-0.04-in-Q1-2024/
4. https://cfohub.com/what-is-a-good-gross-profit-margin/
5. https://www.bloomberg.com/news/articles/2024-02-05/palantir-reports-first-profitable-year-citing-big-ai-demand
6. https://downloads.rivian.com/2md5qhoeajym/1TJ6otGQ8dmSyIi0sh-stum/3f443d04053237a398665ae3dd4a79dd/EX_-_99.2_2Q24_Share-holder_Letter_Final.pdf
7. https://www.marketwatch.com/story/rivians-stock-drops-more-than-7-as-ev-makers-quarterly-loss-balloons-173246b4

Use Market Orders When Buying Stocks, And Here's Why...
1. https://www.zdnet.com/article/intel-takes-minority-stake-in-cmg/
2. https://www.encyclopedia.com/economics/encyclopedias-almanacs-transcripts-and-maps/cmgi-inc
3. https://en.wikipedia.org/wiki/GeoCities

You're the Analyst
1. James Cramer, *Real Money*, Simon & Schuster, 2005

How to Sell Stocks
1. https://rothcocpa.com/trend/fighting-the-last-war/
2. https://en.wikipedia.org/wiki/Krispy_Kreme
3. https://www.cnbc.com/2024/07/24/ceo-turned-employees-into-million-aires-after-selling-tech-startup.html

What to Do When a Stock is Down?
1. https://investor.gopro.com/press-releases/press-release-details/2014/Go-

NOTES ━━━━━━━━━━━━━━━━

Pro-Announces-Pricing-of-Initial-Public-Offering/default.aspx

Don't Be Afraid To Sell Your Dumpster Fires
1. https://www.umass.edu/preferen/You%20Must%20Read%20This/Barber-Odean%202011.pdf

What's The Lesson of Blackberry?
1. https://www.blackberry.com/us/en/company/investors/faq

Determining a "Nosebleed" Valuation
1. https://www.investopedia.com/rivian-ipo-what-happened-and-why-it-matters-5209505
2. https://www.forex.com/en/news-and-analysis/rivian-ipo-everything-you-need-to-know-about-rivian/
3. https://www.statista.com/statistics/225326/amount-of-cars-sold-by-general-motors-worldwide/
4. https://www.statista.com/statistics/297315/ford-vehicle-sales/
5. https://techcrunch.com/2020/08/24/a-quick-peek-at-snowflakes-ipo-filing/
6. https://www.cnbc.com/2020/09/16/snowflake-snow-opening-trading-on-the-nyse.html
7. https://www.gainy.app/ipo/snowflake-ipo-review
8. https://www.nasdaq.com/articles/1-artificial-intelligence-ai-stock-warren-buffett-owns-that-you-may-want-to-buy-hand-over

More on Nosebleeds
1. https://insight.factset.com/sp-500-reporting-a-lower-year-over-year-net-profit-margin-for-the-7th-straight-quarter

Use Market Orders When Buying Stocks
1. https://www.zdnet.com/article/intel-takes-minority-stake-in-cmg/
2. https://www.encyclopedia.com/economics/encyclopedias-almanacs-transcripts-and-maps/cmgi-inc
3. https://en.wikipedia.org/wiki/GeoCities

ETFs Versus Mutual Funds
1. https://smartasset.com/investing/mutual-fund-expense-ratio

How Can I Find ETFs?
1. https://www.statista.com/statistics/278249/global-number-of-etfs/

Can I Buy a Fund that Owns the S&P 500?
1. https://www.investopedia.com/articles/markets/101415/4-best-sp-500-index-funds.asp
2. https://www.etf.com/channels/sp-500-etfs

Is the S&P 500 a High Bar?
1. https://money.usnews.com/investing/term/sp500
2. https://www.msci.com/www/blog-posts/small-caps-have-been-a-big/03951176075
3. https://www.cnbc.com/2023/12/08/investing-pro-why-its-a-fantastic-time-to-add-small-and-mid-caps.html
4. Jeremy Siegel, *Stocks for the Long Run*, McGraw Hill, 2014
5. https://awealthofcommonsense.com/2024/06/is-the-small-cap-premium-dead/

The Simplest Equity Investment You Can Make
1. https://investor.vanguard.com/mutual-funds/profile/portfolio/vtsmx
2. https://www.marketwatch.com/story/vanguard-employees-wont-have-sp-500-funds-in-the-401k-plan-2018-06-06

Seeking Alpha: ETFs That Have Beaten the S&P 500
1. https://finance.yahoo.com/news/chart-day-magnificent-7-stocks-233626055.html
2. https://www.wsj.com/finance/stocks/its-the-magnificent-sevens-market-the-other-stocks-are-just-living-in-it-5d212f95
3. https://www.cnn.com/cnn-underscored/money/magnificent-7-stocks
4. https://www.mellon.com/insights/insights-articles/a-closer-look-at-magnificent-seven-stocks.html
5. https://polarsemi.com/blog/blog-semiconductor-chips-in-a-car/
6. https://www.wsj.com/articles/SB10001424053111903480904576512250915629460
7. https://a16z.com/why-software-is-eating-the-world/

THE SHARK INVESTOR

Should I Try and Time the Market?
1. https://www.businessinsider.com/time-in-the-market-not-timing-the-market-2014-11
2. https://www.cnbc.com/2021/03/24/this-chart-shows-why-investors-should-never-try-to-time-the-stock-market.html
3. https://www.dimensional.com/ca-en/insights/stock-gains-can-add-up-after-big-declines

Dollar Cost Averaging
1. https://www.plansponsor.com/use-index-funds-401ks-increasing/

How to Get Rich Without Really Trying!
1. https://www.regenesys.net/reginsights/the-eighth-wonder-of-the-world-compounding-interest
2. https://pictureperfectportfolios.com/learning-from-warren-buffett-the-power-of-compound-interest/

Do I Need to Invest in International Stocks?
1. https://www.fidelity.com/viewpoints/investing-ideas/international-investing-myths
2. https://www.businessinsider.com/personal-finance/average-stock-market-return
3. https://novelinvestor.com/international-stock-market-performance/
4. https://tradingeconomics.com/japan/stock-market
5. https://www.lazyportfolioetf.com/world-country-indexes-returns/#google_vignette

Investing is Hard!
1. https://www.indexologyblog.com/2021/05/12/equity-diversity-and-inclusion/
2. https://www.morningstar.com/columns/rekenthaler-report/how-many-stocks-beat-indexes
3. https://www.kiplinger.com/investing/stocks/603777/30-best-stocks-of-the-past-30-years

More BAD News
1. https://ritholtz.com/2005/09/djia-1966-1982/

NOTES

"Stern's Law"
1. John Train, *The Money Masters*, HarperPerennial, 1980

Efficient Market Hypothesis
1. https://efinancemanagement.com/investment-decisions/efficient-market-hypothesis
2. http://www.e-m-h.org/Malkiel2005.pdf
3. Burton Malkiel, *A Random Walk Down Wall Street*, W.W. Norton, 2020
4. Ben Mezrich, *The Accidental Billionaires*, Anchor Books, 2010

THE SHARK INVESTOR

INDEX

THE SHARK INVESTOR

ABOUT THE AUTHOR

Michael Stern is a Registered Investment Adviser in Massachusetts, and the founder of Arlington Investment Advisors. He holds the Series 65 Investment Adviser's License.

Mr. Stern was the Publisher and Editor of the *Massachusetts Investor's Digest*, the *Massachusetts Technology Stock Guide*, and the *U.S. Venture Capital & Private Equity Database*.

As a publisher and journalist, Mr. Stern has interviewed top CEOs such as Bob Davis of Lycos and Michael Ruettgers of EMC; as well as portfolio managers, venture capitalists, equity analysts, and startup CEOs.

As an Investment Adviser, Mr. Stern manages assets for individual clients and teaches the courses "Wall Street Bootcamp" and "The Shark Investor."

Mr. Stern lives in the suburbs of Boston with his wife and two children.